THE
GOD
OF
MANY FACES

ANGELO D. MORTIMER

PUBLISHER
Junk@noo Publications and Consulting
Valdosta, GA

Junk@noo Publications and Consulting
www.junkanoopublications.com
Valdosta, GA. 31605

229-234-2306

Copyright © 2021 Angelo D. Mortimer
www.theauthorofthepeople.com
All rights reserved.

All rights reserved solely by the author. The author guarantees all contents are original and do not infringe upon the legal rights of any other person or work. No part of this book may be reproduced in any form without the permission of the author. The views expressed in this book are not necessarily those of the publisher.

Printed in the United States of America.

ISBN: 978-0-578-85943-9

****
Book Cover Design:
Artistic Expressions
Melvin McClanahan Jr.
Hampton, GA 30228
954.646.9973

Editor:
Angelo D. Mortimer

Dedication

This book is especially dedicated to the Most-High from whom all my blessings flow. Without God nothing is possible. *Amen.*

To my mother, Eunice Isaacs-Mortimer or "Pinkey," *I thank you for your endless love and support. A young man could never have asked for a better "mommy." Love you to the sun, moon, and stars.*

To my father, Donald Mortimer, *your undying love, and guidance are deeply etched on the tablet of my heart. You are the best "daddy."*

"Mommy and daddy," it is said that *"Behind every good man is a good woman."* Your teamwork, as parents, proved that.

To my only brother, Darmeeko Isaacs, *I still do not like you since you broke my first toy – kidding. Thank you for being a pillar of wisdom, and always being there when I need you. I love you, big brother.*

To my dashing nephew, Triston Isaacs, and my "boldly-beautiful" niece, Khaleesi Isaacs, *always acknowledge God, no matter where the journey of life takes you. "Unk" loves you two, infinitely.*

In Memoriam

To my second mother, **Val Martinborough nee Isaacs** – my dearly departed: *Thank you for being such a spectacular aunt to me until that sad day you were laid to rest. This accomplishment will have been more special had you lived to witness it. I know you would have been so proud of me. I loved you then, even more now, and forever.*

To my dearly departed, **Louis Isaacs Jr.,** my Uncle Junior: *I was devastated when I learned that you passed recently. You always pushed me to write and be the best I could be. I dreamed about the day you would hold a copy of this book because you loved to read. You are gone too soon. Thank you for impressing upon me that, "a daisy could never be a rose." I miss and love you so much, but my peace is that I gave you your flowers here among the living.*

To **Otilio Joseph,** whom I called, "Brother Joe" or "Brojo," my dearly departed: *A family friend and father figure indeed, you were an amazing human and gentleman. Your biggest appeal to me up until your death was, "Lo, never forget God." I promised, I won't Brojo, I won't. This is my homage to your unforgettable memory.*

Special Acknowledgement

To all my family, close friends, and acquaintances around the world, too numerous to mention, *thank you from the bottom of my heart for your love.*

To my sponsors, *a special thank you for your generous donations in support of my publishing efforts.*

To Dr. Michelle Bain, my former English Lecturer at The University of The Bahamas, here is your moment. *Thank you for igniting my gift of expression. I appreciate you.*

I recognize:

    Cousin "Angie" Farquharson-Bruey
    Glenise Rolle
    Flora Lewis
    Cecilee "CeJay" Hilton
    Nouria Igbinobaro
    Toneika "Barbie" Russell
    Jasmine Lotmore
    Dave Newbold
    Treneille "Tré" Hanna
    Alyssa Sobiech
    Brendalee "Mickey" Donaldson
    Derekia Hepburn
    Aaron Frith Sr.
    Karen Wilson
    Audra "Aunty AC" Cole et al.

Thank you, especially, for being my backbone and the needed encouragement when I felt most overwhelmed during this writing endeavor. You have been most supportive, and for that, I love each of you so much.

Foreword

"Opinion striking against opinion ignites the spark of eloquence."
The Late King George VI

Life is a gift from the Almighty. It was meant to be so peaceful, but the moment we, as humans, begin to label the Most-High we fight on shaky grounds of opinions concerning a Creator we cannot see. At the heart of this conflict is the need to understand that the world forms a unique tapestry joined together by events of the past either victorious or evil.

There is fact and there is opinion. Fact is truth beyond a reasonable doubt. It cannot be seen another way. Opinions are points of view which can change. Religion stands on "personal truth." So, my truth might differ from your truth, and if we discuss them, they become opinions. If religion is "personal", "faith-based" and not a "universal truth", can we really disagree to agree if we are so correct and "know it all"?

This work supports the view that all religions, together, possess the universal truth and the truth rests in peace, love and understanding each other. Religions should all be valued as a library of unique expressions of humanity in relation to the Source.

Human beings are created to coexist, not to create war. When religious war begins, it is not a result of the various religions, it is due to the mercilessness of the people who believe in them. I should like to think that our

Universal Creator who I identify as God, just as you might identify as Allah like our brother or sister identifies as Brahma would destroy us if He were so merciless, stubborn, and unforgiving.

It could not be that anyone outside my religion is damned to hell or simply incorrect for their belief. I am thankful to Jehovah that He has enlightened me beyond casting that type of judgment on others when I am neither appointed to that position nor hold that authority to do so. That is solely God's responsibility.

Those who judge are hellishly out of order. I am overjoyed that my true circle of family and friends has assisted me in pursuing a more constructive set of beliefs in addition to my Christian perspective. I encourage the world to come together in love.

I have had countless conversations through the years that are most memorable, but one such discussion engaged an indescribable passion within me to write this book. My friend, Dave Newbold, and I were having a chat one day and I happened to suggest that there are so many sides to God. I randomly blurted, *"Dave, He is a God of Many Faces!"*

The moment I made that statement, Dave practically pleaded that I repeat myself. When I did, he replied, *"I love that,"* and encouraged me to write a book about the message. I take this time to say, thank you, Dave.

Moreover, the initial name of this book was, *"God of Many Faces."* It then changed to, *"Our God of Many Faces."* Yet, the words *"Our God"* are personal which can suggest that the Creator is specifically found in one religion. This, regrettably, in my opinion, is not the case.

God made us all. And so, the permanent name of this book became, *"The God of Many Faces."* The word "the" is definitive and signifies supremacy, unity, and inclusivity. Such elements are required for global understanding, love, and peace which in turn, promote religious tolerance worldwide.

Conclusively, this book is my best attempt to present a little of who I am, the way God revealed Himself to me, and a summary of His wonder and aspects of God that is common across religious divides. The intention is not to offend, but rather to appeal to the hearts of mankind which can stimulate global togetherness.

The truth is often difficult to accept, but it sets the captive free. What imprisons the masses is the unwillingness to accept the possibility that all manner of knowledge is uniquely that.

My charge to humanity is that we are not required to agree with others as far as religion goes but we should respect each other, because all human thoughts are valid – we all have a story.

No one on Earth is a child of a lesser God because God, or whatever we call or perceive Him to be is the Creator of us all. Wouldn't you agree?

Table of Contents

Born to Be Peculiar	1
Awesome Encounters	18
God Emerged	40
Simply Profound	65
His Omnipotence	84
And Omniscience	101
God is Omnipotent, Omniscient and Most Omnipresent	120
Affirming the Most High	142
The Thing about Organized Religion	150
The Most-High Above all Religions	164
My Spiritual Journey	174
The Creator – A Spirit	185
Agape – A Love like No Other	193
Most Benevolent and Merciful	203
Our God Avenges	213
Jehovah - The Just	223
The Color of God	233
God Created with Purpose	246
A Master of Time	257
The Author and Finisher of our Fate	270

CHAPTER ONE
Born to Be Peculiar

People find me strange. Strange is good. It represents individuality – that which is unique. Experience taught me that people think of anything that is not easily understood as precisely that – strange.

At the age of twenty-three, I began coining the quote, *"Life is an endless drama of music and words."* Poetic isn't it? It came from a truly deep place at a time in my life when I felt I went through enough in the name of growth. Just perhaps you will come to understand why I happily embrace the title of being spectacularly peculiar – thank you.

Understand that I am a Christian believing in one Universal Creator. I call Him God. I believe that He sent His Beloved Son, Christ Jesus, as a living sacrifice into our world of sin, so that its citizens will have hope on a path that leads to freedom. I believe in the Holy Spirit and that it brings comfort and confirmation.

While I claim Christianity as my religion, having been raised as an Anglican, I oppose *"organized religion to the exclusion of others"* because I do not believe that it is the only path to salvation. I believe this discovery has brought me to a deeper, worldwide understanding. Notice I affirm the words, "worldwide" and "understanding." They are important. I believe, from the depths of my soul, that understanding is the bridge to peace since attempting to understand others regardless of race, nationality, religion, sexual orientation, and all things debatable promotes unity.

The sword of tolerance attracts everything that is necessary for rich experiences as we coexist as humans. This requires love at the root.

I attempt to touch your heart, the heart of a beautiful soul, even if you were never told those words enough. I ask Spirit, that which is Holy, that which is pure, to destroy all spirits that are negative and wrong. I speak to the Collective, all that is good, be them the angels, spiritual guides, conscience and morality, the wisdom of my ancestors through their past wisdom and deeds beyond a curse – the signs and wonders, seen and unseen. God guide me.

As time rewinds, I can hear my first cries. I was gifted to a strong woman who at the time, could not recognize how much she would truly come to love me. Indeed, I was cute as a button. You could not tell my Aunt Val, my mother's favorite sister any different. The strong evidence can be found in the photographs that I saw throughout my childhood.

"Mommy," known to others as "Pinkey," did not see anything cute; she saw a frog. To this day I "squawk" whenever I think about it. But I do not blame her because she suffered what many mothers experience after giving birth. Post-Partum Depression is not a pretty situation for mothers and their newborns. At least I was spared any trauma and survived. I have heard of babies that were not so fortunate due to violence or even death.

"Daddy," or Donald, and to some, "the Plumber." has also been a true blessing to me. He was quite the needed balance in terms of discipline when I was a little boy since he is stricter than mommy, who was always more easy-going. Mommy did not lie on Donald Mortimer; we both have huge noses!

Aunt Val was appointed my second mother and named me, Angelo, since mommy was unprepared to be bothered with her baby frog. I was named Angelo because Aunt Val felt, in her words, that *"I looked like a little angel with something to say."* I do not believe I bonded with mommy during my initial moments here on Earth, and so it only followed that Aunt Val would play a special role in my upbringing until her death at the age of forty-nine.

Please do not call me DeAngelo. I am wearing the biggest grin and laughing so loud, it could awaken anyone from the grip of a coma. In The Bahamas, as Bahamians can attest, there are many DeAngelos, so I find myself having to correct my countrymen from committing this harmless crime against my person. I am laughing now even more hysterically, but I digress.

Angelo, in the Italian language means *"Messenger."* It is the masculine form for *"angel,"* whose responsibility in the Bible included delivering messages, acting as guides, as well as warriors depending on their rank and type.

Discussing my name from a Christian perspective, it is appropriate for a Prophet. A Prophet is one who can declare messages as received from God. These messages are called prophecies or oracles, and they would appear to be psychic. Now psychic messages are deemed occult to Christians and are associated with divination. I am not moved to carry out a deep discussion on those perspectives other than to mention that prophecies are mandated to edify, encourage, and comfort the church. While people might define the church as the building where worshippers meet, the church is the worshippers themselves. This includes all peoples, as our bodies are meant to be the temples in which the spirit lives.

Christianity will also reveal a very sad truth for the Prophet, which is we are not commonly liked in our township or country for that matter. How can we truly be liked or even accepted when we are appointed to speak truth? Truth for many is good when it is comfortable to hear. But the "bad truth" is the uncomfortable truth that most people strongly dislike. Frankly, the truth hurts. Straight!

In my own faith, I see many Prophets who are spot on in terms of what they see, but they somehow are paid as if it is a job. The Prophet has not been created for a profit – period! Prophets can be blessed by others without expecting or even asking for it but should not give edification and encouragement and comfort for the Almighty dollar. Again, the Prophet should reap no profit!

Indeed, from an early age, I began to face some very interesting scenarios, which at the time, I did not understand. But now I realize that it is a gift. I must admit that, oftentimes, what I see is not razor-sharp like some Prophets I know. But, interestingly, the visions happen, or they link to some form of encouragement or motivation. I do not think of myself as better than any other human on Earth. In fact, I do not crave the title, Prophet, because the gift is granted with an awesome responsibility to impact the world. I will never forget my first dream as a child that happened in such an amazing way.

I could not be more than twelve years old. I knew nothing about relationships. The only thing I understood was that tingly feeling children experience in matters involving little boys liking little girls and vice versa. I could not reasonably understand the nature of cheating or having affairs. I was too young for that. My brain had to explain it to mommy because I knew something strange was going to happen.

I did not understand it. I simply knew it. I told mommy about one of many strange dreams and expressed it like a child. It involved an adult scandal that surfaced at a Bible study group. Mommy could only rebuke me and fired back that it was only a dream. She knew what prophecy was, but she did not believe then that I could see events before they happen. To this day my mother is not a fan of prophecy.

What was even more uncomfortable about what I revealed is that the new and mysterious mistress was related to the Ministry Leader where we worshipped. Mommy would not carry that burden and she told the leader what I dreamed.

I remember the leader's strange reaction – her stare – when she found out. The leader said nothing and to this day, I remain unsure whether it was a sign of disbelief or betrayal – the very possibility that she knew what was going on.

She always told mommy that I was special. Indeed, the couple wound up breaking up, and the gentleman concerned married the mistress – facts! That dream was the beginning of many dreams and visions that surfaced during my lifetime.

Essentially, I should explain that mommy is a very serious Christian. She is open to other faiths and philosophies but stands firm on the teachings of Christianity and her belief that God is real. One thing I love about mommy, though, is that she took me on her spiritual journey, but always allowed me to think for myself. She encouraged my spiritual development by relaxing the claws of tradition. Thus, I could appreciate different religious perspectives as mommy addressed those confusing questions to strengthen my understanding. Being an amazing mother, she merely grounded my understanding not always knowing the answer, but was always moved to find out.

There was a time when I would go to the Anglican Church. It was so "boujee" and most appropriate for the saints and holiest of holies. It felt so "Church of England" even though, back then, I did not know what it meant to be British. I felt out of place, honestly. A child dropping half asleep to degrees of an all-out faint, that would be me. I only began to appreciate that type of worship more recently as an adult and understandably so.

Now outside the traditional Anglican mass, I could be seen trailing behind mommy, and sometimes daddy, to some prayer meeting or Bible study. My encounters there were much more "relatable." There were fewer rituals so to speak. People would praise with a strong passion, cry loudly, and speak a strange language. Thus, I experienced the windchill of worship so young.

Coupled with this sensational side of God, mommy always explained the faces of worship in a way a child could understand. I grew to appreciate the solemn approach of burning incense and repeating chant-like rituals in front of the altar compared to the "Jumper Church" where people are free to "let loose." Liberal churches are very different because there is freedom that is untied since spirits, whether good or bad, can be expressed with passion in so many unique ways. I enjoyed joining a church-inspired Conga line and to be honest, it nurtured within me a more practical sense of God.

What is more is that from an early age I had been applying an aspect of the Law of Attraction and was totally unaware. I firmly believe one's upbringing is extremely crucial to the way one sees life and gets through it. The Law of Attraction has many layers, but one of my favorites is the notion that when we think positively that something will happen to the point of seeing it, it will actually happen.

There is a difference though. Believing something will happen and knowing something will happen are both strong examples of faith. When you believe, there is arguably some doubt left; when you know, how can you question it? For example, if I believe John Doe is my father – I still have doubt because Jack could be daddy too. If I know John is my father, he is daddy – period.

I will never forget the first Roger and Hammerstein movie I watched called, "The Sound of Music" filmed in Salzburg, Austria. Then came, "Mary Poppins," "My Fair Lady," "Fiddler on The Roof," "Chitty-Chitty-Bang-Bang," "State Fair," "The Shirley Temple Collection" and many more.

Relevant to the Law of Attraction, I remember watching the Sound of Music, and as I sang along, I could see myself doing the same things as the characters and visualizing myself there. I remember watching, "My Fair Lady" and thinking to myself that I was a character living during those nostalgic times in England where I was among the upper class because I spoke well. I always saw myself going there someday.

Surprisingly, this shaped the way I say words. A lot of people still ask if I am a Bahamian. I smile most of the time because I speak what I practiced once from a television screen. The day would come that my childish imagination became true. So, what does a believer of any opposing religion say to this? The Law of Attraction is arguably more philosophy or scientific than it is religious because it encompasses the Universe and affirmation. Am I sinner? I mean the Bible does say that "if you have faith as small as a mustard seed, you could move mountains."

By virtue of believing the possible and to some impossible, I would go to Europe. It is hoped that you find the story inspirational. I could remember a schoolmate addressing a room full of Senior High School students. I attended a private school, and we would assemble on Fridays at what the school simply called, "Assembly."

It was a cute expression, I think. In the instance of having to use the bathroom wherein time was short, and an accompanying classmate had to attend, I would simply say, "I have got to use the restroom; see you at Assembly."

I enjoyed Assembly because it was there that schoolmates heard of everything related to student life and special recognition was given to pupils who deserved it. We also had the occasional guest speaker, and as I recall, we met up for thirty to forty-five minutes every Friday. My memories have faded, but I vaguely remember walking in a single file with my male classmates to wherever we would be meeting on that given Friday.

There she was, Katarvia Taylor, my classmate Kataran Taylor's sister. She was beaming since she had recently participated in a Foreign Youth Exchange Program to Ecuador becoming fluent in Spanish. Despite being a dreamy student, Katarvia's enthusiasm caught my attention. Her clear happiness and gratitude for what she called a very life-changing experience and overall delivery sparked my interest in the program. I knew that I wanted that kind of adventure.

When I went home, I could remember telling mommy and daddy about the program and asking them if I could go. Mommy didn't see a reason why not and of course daddy would agree. Mommy told me to find out more information and go after my dreams. I must have been in the eleventh grade. I had such a strong determination that I would be going that I once again could smell the destination; I could feel and see myself there – eating and greeting in an unknown environment with unknown people mouthing words in their unknown language.

The big day finally came. I was taking deep breaths as a woman experiencing labor. There were over a hundred applicants to win this prestigious scholarship. Only three would be selected. I was brimming with anticipation and overanalyzing as usual – in cold sweat. Butterflies were dancing in my belly. I felt sick. Yet I knew that I had to give it my all to have a fighting chance.

My name is called. I walk through the door and nearly fell down a few times because my legs felt light and incapable of supporting my weight. I cannot remember the exact number of panelists, but I am sure at least three sat with emotionless faces. There seemed to be no time for laughter. I was up for the trial of my life in front of the fiercest cross examiners. That is how they made me feel.

The first question was asked, and I briefly went blank to a bladder moment. I thought to myself, "Why do I feel like I cannot answer this"? I felt stupid, but drew inner strength and recall asking for the question to be repeated. And whatever the question was, it had been repeated by a panelist. And then I repeated it aloud answering to the best of my ability. I tried my usual charm to break the seriousness of my environment. But every time I tried, the pink elephant increasingly grew bigger.

As the questions fired, I answered. I did my best. Each time the looks seemed uglier and an immense feeling of defeat came over me, not because I was not responding with full explanation, but the examiners seemed unimpressed or showed no feeling that they understood my answers. My last question was complete. I politely thanked the panel, but if I were a dog, a wagging tail would be curling up between hind legs on my way out.

I exited the interview for what seemed like an eternity. Mommy then took for what seemed to be another eon to pick me up! When asked how the interview went, I blurted a response in a rage of defeat. I felt so disappointed in myself. I thought I lost a golden opportunity, and my world was crumbling – I failed. I suffered a "Mission Collapsed." Now those who know me well call me dramatic. I agree. Looking back at it, I would have been an excellent hopeful for the Soap Opera, "The Day Angelo Dies." Even if told otherwise, I would not believe it. I was a classic perfectionist. Mommy assured me that I might have done much better than I thought. I forgot about it because I was too hard on myself. I allowed negativity to set in to erase the thought that I would be going anywhere.

Some weeks later a gentleman who oversaw the interview called our home phone and I answered. He greeted me plainly without really mentioning the program. He merely said hello and asked to speak to mommy. When I passed the phone to her, I knew it was to say thanks for my participation and my options for being a possible candidate for the program the following year.

Then mommy, in mid conversation, informed me that I was chosen among the top three to go that year. I was overjoyed and felt a wave of shock horror throughout my body. I could not decide how to let it out. I finally gave a confused reaction of intense happiness near orgasm.

Mommy could tell I was happy and told the Administrator that I honestly believed that I would not be chosen for the scholarship. To my surprise, he stated that I was selected by the time I walked out. He admitted that my answers blew the panelists away and they were impressed to know that I thought so deeply at my age. Honestly, I was no "A" student in school, but the news made me feel so Valedictorian. Some months passed and a planned camping trip somewhere in Florida was mandatory to find out the country to which I would be sent for an entire year of my life.

"Thailand?" I must have repeated that country ten times before it finally sank. I knew I did not want to go there. I had not graduated yet during which at the actual graduation ceremony I was given the Overall Spanish Award for highest cumulative score in Spanish of the graduating class. I highlighted on my application that I wanted to go to a Spanish-speaking country. I was not being discriminatory. I do not even think it was about the destination. I simply did not want to go to Thailand or the old Siam regardless of it being dubbed, "The Land of Smiles."

There were three of us Bahamians, out of over a hundred applicants, who were assigned to a country – two girls and me. One girl was selected to go to Brazil and the next to Sweden. I asked to switch with the girl going to

Brazil since Brazilian Portuguese is like Spanish, but she refused. The other assigned to Sweden found herself in my dilemma because she did not want to go there. She felt that it would be too cold. I asked if she would be willing to go to Thailand because Europe was my second choice. It was an automatic swap since the girl's dream was to see Asia. The arrangements became final.

At last! It was high school graduation. I could remember my journey to the unknown getting closer as I sit on cloud 9. Everything was beginning to come true as I had seen it as a child. Understanding Law of Attraction provided some deep insight, received more recently, since back then I was oblivious to the power of positive thoughts.

Manifestation was responsible for that moment at Miami International Airport where in my mind I could not believe that my dream was finally happening. The flight was announced. Meanwhile reality is kicking in. To see my mommy fighting to be brave, when I knew deep inside, she was falling apart, made me so sad. It was touching enough to make my mind change from going anywhere. For a second there, I nearly broke down; I was prepared to let go of everything for which I worked so hard. In addition, fear began to creep in. I started to think about the "strange" decision to meet up with "strangers."

A deeper voice spoke to my fears and told me to keep going. People could be seen giving their tickets to the agent. Mommy and daddy were foot to foot behind me. I grew sadder, but happier at the same time. There were the final hugs before I could feel those warm embraces again for a year. I was next to give my ticket. I gave a last smile, that final goodbye, assuring my parents that I would see them soon and that I loved them so much.

At that moment when I turned around, I knew my heart was aching. I knew I had to be brave and so I walked to the airplane boldly. I knew I could run back into the arms of my parents who, deep down, would not discourage it. Yet how do I make memories if I do not take the leap of faith? How do I recall good times if I refuse to plunge into unknown waters?

I walked a while and was eventually seated on an aircraft headed to Chicago. The door finally shut. I knew it was over. Not my life, though. What ended was the opportunity to be afraid. There I was in deep reflection as the airplane taxi, and before I knew it many souls aboard were airborne. I fell asleep.

I arose from blackness to a rough landing on a foreign soil. The flight could not have been any more than two hours and forty-five minutes. The ride to the arrival gate took forever confirming that Chicago O'Hare is the busiest airport in the United States. As I walked with my hand luggage through the terminal, I broke out in a cold sweat. I was lost and overwhelmed. I had no sense of direction and people were walking so fast to catch their flights. I was alone on a journey that was beginning to frighten me. As though he were a guardian angel, some random airport worker must have sensed that I needed some assistance. I told him that I did not know where my gate was when he asked if I was okay. He realized that I was running late the moment he reviewed my ticket and told me to follow him and to be quick about it.

I followed. He led me in the right direction pointing me further down the way I should go. I had to take a tram, and thankfully, it was caught in the nick of time. I managed to make my flight by the stroke of luck. Imagine me. I was last aboard and last to my seat on my first ever transatlantic flight. I would be flying to Stockholm Arlanda Airport for nine hours.

The first language spoken over the microphone was Swedish. It made me laugh like a hyper chimpanzee. Thank heavens for the English translation that gave me a moment to breathe. I was very tired but slept a bit despite being awakened to eat meals a few times during flight. I watched some in-flight entertainment to keep me occupied when I was not asleep. Then eventually the much-anticipated descent into Sweden had come. I was welcomed by the fjords and glaciers way below as I looked out of the aircraft window. The air became thinner. It was a different world.

This time the landing was a lot smoother. For those who have travelled to Sweden or will in the future, Stockholm Arlanda is agreeably a large space where aircrafts are parked. It is like a town out yonder, so to be picked up by your host, you must catch a train to meet them. When I arrived at the airport, I met my first host father, Hans. He was excited to meet me. I fell asleep several times during the drive home. We drove for hours. I managed to see some townships headed to Hudiksvall which was soon to be my new home.

I left The Bahamas in the summer of August 2000. Yet, I wondered how was it that I was still feeling the chill of Bahamian winter? How is it that Swedes are wearing shorts and short T-shirts? It was so weird to me. However, it was not to them because it is Arctic summer and it never really gets very hot in Scandinavia, just as it never gets too cold in The Bahamas, the country in which I was born.

We approached Hudiksvall in the province of Dalarna. The lush green and wildflowers made the scene awful-picturesque. Most homes were wooden and of a dark, maroon red, trimmed with white. On some homes there might be a bit of blue, but it was rare. My new surroundings looked like a page from a fairy tale and that is how I described my new environment to mommy on that first call to say that I arrived safely. Indeed, it was the home of the cartoon character, Pippi Longstocking.

Eventually I met my host mother who was very warm, as she hugged and welcomed me to my new home. I also met my host brother, Daniel, who would be leaving for Ohio to complete his exchange year. My little cute host sister was seven at the time with the purest blue eyes. Her first words in Swedish and translated were, "My name is Yanna, (Anna) – welcome." The reason Anna remains so special to me is she helped me learn Swedish. She put labels on different things to pronounce them. This happened during the first several weeks after moving into her home.

Throughout the year, I would experience other host families who taught me important lessons and met people from countries I once read about in books. Random souls taught me that you can travel the world by simply being open-minded and engaging. As an exchange student, I was required to remain as free as possible from wrong ideas to receive others and learn cultural differences. I was expected to jump over cultural shock like a horse at the Equestrian.

The path to the unknown exposed me to stories of people that could make you laugh at the colorful ways they do things, cry, or even wail from the horror experienced causing outrage due to injustices that are unspeakable. That is when I realized that my country, The Bahamas, is quite blessed.

But if you want to be truly knowledgeable, you must be exposed to difference. Then you will come to know that the world is so much bigger than your backyard. You will come to know that you might feel accomplished by part of the truth, but not necessarily the whole truth. One can only be as knowledgeable as the information to which one is open to receive.

When you meet people with a backyard that is different from yours, there is more to learn. One backyard might have a patio and a pool amidst a desert, but no fruit trees. Another backyard might have a guest house with fruit trees and consistently dewy grass. Because they are not the same, does not mean that either is better than the other. What it means is that experiences in both backyards will be different to teach, differently. We are the children of the same Creator. Through our differences, we can appreciate, "The God of Many Faces."

CHAPTER TWO
Awesome Encounters

I arrived – I was there. I was the cat's meow – "the shit." I had finally made it to Sweden. I was breathing with the Swedes; I ate and laughed with them. And I would learn the Swedish language within a wondrous year. It was my goal to dive into such a story-book culture.

Everything for which I worked so hard was allowing me to reap the benefits. All the feelings of being unsuccessful beyond that scary interview made me feel grand. I now could appreciate the fact that I experienced the doubt and the disappointment that made me go hard on myself since, at the end of the day, I leapt, quantum leap, into a fantasy. I merely strived for the best and it taught me that hard work pays off.

Swedish like its quintuplet-sister languages, Danish, Finnish, Norwegian, and Icelandic, are very much rare languages. Exchange students to Sweden were required to attend a language course at a camping ground in a town some hours away from my new hometown. I was so ready! I looked forward to meeting other exchange students from around the world. That would be my passport to different countries of origin.

Speaking to foreigners, whether we realize it or not, provides a glimpse that is not so touristy. Exchange of thoughts and points of view make for a vivid journey. People from different walks are not expected to see things the same way, but there are many ways that humans connect through what is common. It is a powerful fact that we are all individuals in search of purpose, whether consciously or subconsciously, to improve our sense of belonging. We want to know why we are here on Earth.

A question that begs to be answered is which organization was responsible for such a brilliant opportunity. The Rotary Club International deserves this moment. Yearly, it promotes the unifying of young people worldwide through the concept of foreign youth exchange. What is truly unique about the scholarship is that there is not necessarily a direct exchange between participating countries, but rather there is a large network across the globe tearing down borders of division.

I remember that moment when we, the exchange students, first met – it was like a first date. I could feel the excitement churning in the pit of my belly. I remember that train ride like it was yesterday. How could I forget that feeling of being so thrilled that I lost 1,500 Swedish Crowns? At the time it will have totaled just a little less than $150.00. To me I felt I had lost the world. I felt like I was not going to enjoy the experience because I lost my course money. Money talks – point blank!

Interestingly, my carelessness would be the key to a welcome experience. You see everyone else was mature enough not to lose their payment for the course. My sadness exposed a humble side that made me noticeable. It oozed from my vulnerability and innocence – the fact that I was a young, evolving human. I was the only black exchange student from The Bahamas; a country amid a chain of ocean jewels spreading like a charm bracelet across the Atlantic Ocean. It is known to be a faraway place and called, by many, a paradise on Earth.

The underlying spiritual revelation that I came to discover many years later is that God is everywhere. Christianity teaches through scripture that, *"He who God keeps is well kept"* for *"God will never leave the righteous forsaken nor his seed begging bread."* Acts of kindness is of God. A neutral perspective is simply that being Children of the Universe, regardless of what we call our universal Father, makes us entitled to being provided for like the animals. I am a mammal and so are you. If God takes care of the birds of the air, the fishes of our seas, the flowers so vibrantly clear, the animals above the grass to the swaying trees, how can we believe that the Universal Creator will forget us?

Spirit showed up to show off! Spirit showed up so on time that I was able to enjoy those days at the language camp. I was able to engage in making the well-known Dalarhest – a culturally handcrafted horse within the province in which I was residing at the time. God created me awkward enough that I was the only exchange student who required being taught to row a rowboat since I hopelessly rowed in circles. The hilarity was surreal. My crowning moment was that I, the eclectic island boy, who lost his money, became head of the Swedish class. I soaked up the basics of my new language like a sponge. God uses the most unlikely of candidates to expose His equality and love for mankind.

Furthermore, God exposed His face through the faces of diversity. We, mere teenagers, resembled the colors of the rainbow. Like on that random night, when two Japanese girls dressed in Kimonos and frightened me with ghostly make up. It was culture night and the time when I learned about the Geisha. I was blown away.

That same night I also learned about the liberties of France because how dare that French girl, Gwen, who would become a good friend of mine, sneak to smoke cigarettes! She did not give a hoot about the Rotary's insistence that there was to be no smoking – never. It was the night I found that Leif was not pronounced "leaf" but "Lay-f" which is actually a boy's name. It was the night I learned that Australians and New Zealanders sound almost identical. It was the night that I realized that a Japanese girl looked cool in pink hair instead of the typical black and that the same girl named "Yo" had a "dudette's" personality which matched her favorite greeting "Yo, sup?" The "Yo - Yo," to my mind that all Asian girls are not so reserved.

It was the night I realized that American whites did not look so "American-white" in our new territory because spiritually there was a link to their ancestors. It was the night I found out that people did not believe in God but rather in a persuasive scientific conviction. Who is an Atheist again?

It was the night that exchange students would understand why I made my exchange pin out of plaited straw and hot-glued a Bahamian postal stamp on it. They came to know, more directly, that I am a descendant of slavery. Rotary pins were exchanged between exchange students as tokens to decorate our Rotarian jackets. The culture of exchange students is to meet and exchange with others across cultures and each pin represented a country. There were countless encounters – simply countless. As we shared our stories, we merely glimpsed another Face of God.

It was time to return home to Hudiksvall and embark on a year's journey. It did not take long. Time is so fleeting that if we allow ourselves to think about it, we will be sad. We might become sad because some experiences we never want to end but they must. There was not a long break between the time that I returned to Hudiksvall and the time that I would start school. I might not remember the exact timeframe that it took between those periods, but the memory of my first day at my new school stands out like a sore thumb. And yes, I graduated from High school back home, in The Bahamas, only to return to High School in Sweden.

I was more accustomed to an unforgiving uniformity at an academic institution – school uniforms are worn where I was born, and you follow the routine or else. Boys were to be dressed in pressed dress pants and a dress shirt neatly tucked in with a belt. I am sure you would want, as an islander, to put on an undershirt because days grew hot and skin became sticky enough to cling to shirts when exposed. Boys avoided wearing dress pants that revealed their socks for fear of being told that they are 'gunin'. This happened when the seam that runs down the middle of both legs makes the bottom stick out like a gun shooting bullets.

Could you imagine taking a seat in that predicament? To add insult to injury, imagine being required to wear a tie in addition to being four-eyed. You can rest assured you would be viciously teased.

Island-black girls grow sexy and shapely just as island-white girls, and even those in between, who might not be as blessed with such endowed parts, blossomed seductively. One thing was certain: the rules were stricter for girls. They had better wear loose fitted skirts usually of plaid fabric when they are young and a plainer fabric when they matured. There was to be no excessive jewelry. In fact, girls were limited only to wearing a watch and gold knobs in their ears. There was to be no dangling or clinking accessories worn. Breaking the rules was expected. Forward girls shortened skirts and opened the top button of their blouses for a peek of their newfound cleavage.

Perhaps Principals caught on when vests were introduced. Buttons of blouses at the throat were buttoned, and an appropriate, more feminine tie was to be worn. Boys and girls were asked to wear polished shoes and the only colors allowed were black and brown. We could wear tennis shoes for Physical Education classes with our P.E. uniforms designed in the spirit of sporting and team identity.

Picture the look of shock on my face as I exited my host father, Hans' car on that first day of school. There was a fog of smoke at the entrance and it was not from a shaft on the roof, but from the mouthpiece of quite the bold human being. He wore the rainbow and lightning combined for his hairstyle. He must have been a Punk Rock Star. If not, he was some hybrid of a porcupine with oil-based colors exploding through his hair. I was unsure if I wanted to enter the building to be attacked by the walking dead. He was pale enough and ever made-up with make-up. It will have been impossible to convince me that he had not represented the entire population on the inside of the school. I was afraid of being bitten and transformed to another zombie.

I blinked and tried to feel like I was somewhere else and somehow gained the strength to tell my host father goodbye and that I would see him after school. I walked toward the entrance and said hello to what I perceived for a moment to be an alien. It was encouraging when I walked indoors. The scenario turned back to normal. I began to see people with whom I could relate. I knew at that point that I could make friends because I was open-minded and friendly. I knew that I could appreciate my new schooling environment for the upcoming year. Despite my confidence, there were incidents that gradually emerged because I was old enough to address them for a change. Perhaps even in a more productive way, I was willing to grow. Not only was I old enough, I chose to relocate for one year under scholarship to pursue a foreign way of life, so of course I could only expect that there were going to be many differences.

Swedish schooling was an engaging experience to say the least. I was already feeling strange since I was wearing such casual clothes, but I loved the newfound liberty. I loved the attention from being a new face – a youth

Ambassador from a far-off place. I loved the new land, the new town, the new school, and of course, the new culture. There were so many precious memories had that they make it impossible to recall them.

I will start with my classmates. It was decided by my Principal who, too, was a Rotarian and my appointed Counselor, that I sit courses in the School of Humanities. Understand that Rotarian Counselors were responsible for resolving any challenges faced by incoming exchange students. I enjoyed my course selection that had been reduced in number because I was to learn in Swedish. I was placed in Swedish Language, Swedish for Immigrants, Drama, Italian, Spanish, Mathematics and English. I dropped Italian eventually because it all became too confusing. My homeroom teacher, Dame Eva Norén, was so charismatic – a riot. She made me feel so welcome; I will never forget her. My class was small; it could not be more than, say, ten of us.

What I truly appreciated about Swedish Secondary Schools is that they place students in classes based upon their strengths. There educational system is unmatched because they give all manner of learning styles a chance. No student is left behind unless there is a willful choice to become nothing. But with all its undoubted positives, I did experience some awkwardness not because it was negative, but I would come to find out that I was simply not accustomed to certain ways of doing things.

Something as simple as taking showers as a student after Physical Education class was a challenge for me. Back in the islands, we did not shower; the most we did was a "cowboy." And if we smelled bad, we were teased until we learned a sensible solution. But Swedish students were trained to take showers. At the time, my new school was already a huge building, but there were the "barracks" since additional classes were being built. Taking showers was not optional even if you had to endure the bitter cold. You showered and "off you go."

My first experience was so embarrassing. I thought I was headed to a place where at least there would be some form of privacy. By then I had made a few friends, but we were barely on speaking terms. I was told where to go to shower after some friendly handball matches which is a popular sport in Sweden.

As I entered with my gym bag and looked up, my neck grew stiff. There I stood speechless because just moments before people seemed normal and appropriately dressed. Now the scene had drastically changed because cloth somehow biodegraded to skin. Guys seemingly so macho during a prior handball match were now smiling in an outright, bald-naked orgy. If eyes could burn, I will have smoked everyone in the room. The one guy with whom I was friendliest approached me penis-first, his eyes locked on mine, and he dangled quite obviously from his birthday suit.

I spun around like a virgin girl who realized she has witnessed mission impossible – gulp and all. Like the time the Spanish boy attempted to kiss me in Spain, and I reacted with the quickness of a Listerine commercial. "No, no, who you kissin' dude?" I was panicked, outraged, and dumbfounded all at once. Looking back at it, I am happy to have had those very odd encounters because what is sexuality to a Swede compared to a Bahamian? The comparison, however, should not be measured in terms of right versus wrong, but rather the measure of cultural norms and how societies measure the acceptable against the unacceptable.

There were special bathrooms built for Swedish and immigrant students who were uncomfortable taking showers in the open due to religious belief. My discomfort arose, conversely, due to cultural belief so I was accommodated. The talk of sexuality is bound to go downhill when minds are closed. Open conversation can become uncomfortable to those who might not be so exposed, culturally, to sexual freedom of expression. I must say sexuality in Sweden, is more fluid.

If you thought those encounters were thrills of shock horror, how about blatant sex in the restroom when I had to take a quick wee. I was so angry. The noises were damn savage. I cursed machine-gun-bullets back then because I was young and carefree. I told them to get the "F" out the way because I had to pee and take that "shit" elsewhere.

The law of sex is seemingly more relaxed in Europe. There might be repression of it by minority groups who have relocated from countries where young ladies hold fists in front of their teeth when smiling for fear of being viewed as promiscuous. Their men, too, might be viewed as heartless to sleep with women since their deeds stain the virgin; a stain within his religion that causes her to be stoned or brings dishonor to her family; a stain that makes him guilty, but does not imprison him because it is best to laugh at sowing wild oats and flat-bury the secret.

Back in the islands, since the topic of sexuality is ripe – biblical scripture commands the married couple not to commit adultery and tells the unwed to avoid fornication. The latter scenario seems a bit more pardonable but discouraged. The Creator is fair as He has created us with a nature that calls to procreate. The balance to repress urges can be seemingly unbearable. Imagine religious consequences that scar and mark eternally whether by being banished or put to death.

There are countries in the world where this is a reality. I did not quite know this until my exchange year erupted by the meeting of souls. I met a girl – a beauty. We became the best of friends. Many from her country are of mahogany shades with pitch black, wavy-kinky hair. They are Arab blacks if I were to explain them the best way I know how. She shared her very sad story. I never knew that there was a country called Eritrea. It was born out of war – t'was religious war because two different Faces of God arose.

But one was not God after all. It was an illusion of God: The Head of Evil. Because she is Muslim, she lost her parents in the fight for religious freedom. She lost sight of her home – her birth right relocating to Sweden, not because she thought it a better place or because she wanted a better way of life, but she moved because the Ethiopia she knew became foreign. It became a choice of foreign worlds.

I met a guy – a handsome fellow. We became the best of friends. Many from his country bear the shade of the sun with sharp noses and pitch-black hair strands of the night. I never knew about the Kurds, but I knew about Iraqis. Iraqis and Kurds are supposed to be the same people. The Kurds, however, were the slaughtered like animals under Saddam Hussein. And those who thrived were mistreated in the name of politics.

I knew a girl – a gorgeous young lady. We became the best of friends. I never knew that just hanging out with a female in some countries required that a male be introduced to the fiancé. Yet that fiancé, being a male, is not required to introduce his bride-to-be to a female he befriends.

You see my friend was Albanian and due to be married soon. Every male that befriends her was to be formally introduced to her fiancé before a friendship could blossom. I thought to myself that boy-meet-girl should not be so serious. Despite my belief, possibly the religious requirement exposes a Face of God. It discourages jealousy and uncertainty at the very root of a budding marriage. There is a liberty in Christianity which promotes marriage, but perhaps a better approach is found in Islam – the religion of Muslims. Therefore, choice of religion should be personal and respected.

Yet, I befriended another girl with whom I shared the best of times, but she was not the typical Muslim. She relocated with her family from Turkey. And, indeed, she made me feel like a Turkey that time when she opened her purse and handed me a purple dildo. She was more focused on finding something she needed. My jaw dropped because it was in the open, *"Girl, what!"* I was not only floored because I was not ready, but also by the thought of where the rather large "thingy" had been. I nearly fainted.

And lastly – I would remain the best of friends with a guy. He was a lady's man and quite the adventurous type. Yes – he was a looker, a Swede; white, blonde-haired and all. I would gain further clarification on the views of an Atheist. I would learn how to accept the fact that people have the right to believe in whatever they want to believe even though it seems unbelievable. I had to learn that my beliefs were my beliefs and that behavior which seemed *"against God"* was only born out of individual faith. I would learn that this same friend could walk through some random graveyard and loudly awaken the dead. You might ask how. To him there is no God – there is no church. The dead are simply dead and buried.

Being raised a Christian where it is often said to let the dead bury the dead, I still became offended that my new friend could be so disrespectful to the dead. However, are they not gone? Just perhaps his apparent disrespect was not so disrespectful at all because a spirit is not buried in the dirt. The flesh merely rots there. And like garbage, the hidden corpse is what remains of whose body is no longer in need of appreciation. Is it so disrespectful from that point of view? Maybe this is another Face of God mouthing that we should indeed *"let the dead bury the dead."*

Furthermore, my friend perhaps mastered the detachment to the dead and simply interprets and relates to the Universal Creator as the Source of Science. My friend should not be judged because he is not a child of a lesser God. Think about it. Is a religiously evil person within any religion closer to The Source than a morally good person without religion?

Many Atheists say they do not believe in any form of God or gods of any religion but acknowledge intelligent design and the power of will. I am beginning to translate "belief" to be a simple declaration against the labeled Sources – those Creators which seems to divide us across religions.

You might ask what exactly is the point being conveyed. The point is God who made us all **resembles all faces of all races**! He is the Creator of diversity. He uses us because He lives in us and we all are the mind of God when we live in our highest good. If God be the Source – the Good, and we search Him daily, then actions which generate the spirit of good is of the Source. In Genesis, scripture states that the human being has power over God's creation. We are the supreme animal – the Homo sapiens – the "wise one." We are like other living things. However, we have been empowered and are guided by the Source in a collective spirit – a collective whole. We are powerful beyond measure when we connect and align ourselves with the Source.

During my exchange year I will never forget the unthinkable brink upon my untimely death, but through it all, God showed His face. I had just finished having a major disagreement with my first host father, Hans, absolutely boiling with rage. I no longer wanted to live under the same roof with the man who I came to respect. He said something, which at that age was perhaps not so harmful looking back at it. Nevertheless, whatever happened ignited a roaring inferno within me that could not be contained.

I could remember packing a backpack with clothes because my desire to leave that house was unwavering. My current size would not permit it, but I was smaller at about eighteen or so. Despite my host mother's appeal that I stay, I was determined that I would leave. I was not angry at my pleasant host mother, but I could not say the same about her husband. It was enough, through childish interpretation, to stimulate my legs out the door and I dare anyone stop me. My parents were back at home in the islands and I was a spicy soul. Only my parents could rule me and that was simply the way it was.

Far from staggering, I knew the general direction of where I was going, but it was nightfall, and everything looks different when it is not daylight. The darkness was perfect to become fearful. In the distance I could see huge dogs. They seemed very big and cunning as they headed toward me.

I was very close to the dogs now and in the moment, I was so angry. I perceived the dogs should move out of the way because I was young and stupid. The world should revolve around me and my rebellion. So, I grabbed a big stone and threw it toward the middle of the pack of dogs – or were they wolves? Shit – yikes! Wolves! The leader of the pack cowered in pain. That is how I escaped the unthinkable. I survived because all the wolves fled having glimpsed the Face of God – fearlessness! He emerges in the best and worst of encounters. One fine lesson I learned from such a close call is that when destiny is fruitful and ordained by the Most-High, nothing can harm you.

I made it to my destination. It was my Counselor's parents' house. They welcomed me and gave my Counselor a call. I spoke to him on the phone briefly explaining what happened. He said that he would get clearer details in the morning and that I should not worry about anything. He further assured me that his parents would take good care of me and they did. My Counselor lived in the outskirts of Hudiksvall in an area called Näsviken so he thought it better to avoid a long roundtrip drive. I took a shower, ate a light meal and was off to bed.

The following morning my Counselor arrived and although a resolution of peacemaking between my host father and I was attempted – it was an epic failure. I was unprepared to return to that family. However, the decision was made for me to reside with my Counselor until another family was found. Living with Counselors is not forbidden, but rather discouraged because if there is an issue that arises with the Counselor, life becomes even more complicated since Counselors should always be unbiased "go-to persons." Thus, I was put on notice that the living arrangement would be temporary.

On a scenic drive, both smooth and luxurious, my Counselor drove a very expensive car. I do not remember the brand car, but I knew it was from a luxury line. It was either a Mercedes Benz or Bimmer or Audi. Whichever the brand, I was green to the fact that my Counselor and his wife were wealthy. My only agenda was to switch to another family at that time, so I was comforted in knowing that all my things were securely packed up in my Counselor's car. I was expected to move to at least three families anyway by the end of my exchange year. The program is designed that way so that exchange students can appreciate wider cultural experiences.

We finally pulled up to a road that made my Counselor turn the car wheel. It was a driveway apparently, but my new home was far hidden. We kept driving. And then I saw it. Yes … it was no house. It could not be a motel. It was not big enough. It could not be just a regular house. It was not small enough. It was a mansion. The wealthier in Sweden own such mansions that are generational. I was overwhelmed. All I could do was get my luggage and try to grasp this incredible transition to my new home for the time being.

I was welcomed by my new host mother. She was absolutely stunning, and I could not even disagree when she told me some time later that she was a former Swedish model. I also met two very large dogs, a male and female duo, and they were so human. I was taken to my room, and as I walked around, I was blown away by the spaciousness of the living areas that made two very large dogs look like toy poodles. I entered my bedroom, and in that moment, I must have been crowned a prince.

Large paintings hung on the walls of classic Swedish art. The strokes of oil on canvas made me feel like royalty. Every string instrument that I could ever imagine fit neatly in that room in a strategic corner by a lone chair on legs. In the middle of the bedroom was a pool table. There was only one window, but it was large and tall enough to encourage the breezy arctic air and warming sunlight to enter. My bed was not very large; it was instead very comfortable.

I saw the concerned Face of God. I could only imagine how calming it would be if I could only see it. I felt His warmth and compassion because I was protected. It is agreeable that my decision to leave my first host family was outright reckless, yet I am sure that Jehovah could understand how I felt. He kept me safe and provided safety. The Creator shows up on time and every time.

I could remember, a few months prior, being invited to a neighbor's winter home back at my first host family. They were not only neighbors, but close friends of that host family. They had a lovely home and always were so kind when I went over. I accepted the invitation to go. Just as God protected me from the pack of wolves, He again spared my life from a near fatal crash involving elks roaming in the middle of the road like arrogant wildebeests of the night! Many Swedes die yearly because elks have no sense of direction or care in the world. They merely form random pathways on their journey anywhere. Just animal-retarded!

Everyone in the car was thrilled to be going to the slopes to ski. The car heater was on full blast because it was bitterly cold. I could see the frost on the windshield, but I could not foresee that looking at my friend for a brief moment would frighten me enough to scream, "Look out!" We swerved and spun uncontrollably for eons of what I felt were flashes of my life being stolen before my very eyes. It was a complete loss of control. When it was all over, I could see God's Face. The face that mouthed that He is in control. I could feel His presence. Spirit assured me that nothing could happen to me unless the Creator agrees.

Hindsight is always 20/20, yet the strength of the lessons learned depends on one's spiritual maturity. For example, when I initially survived the experience, I merely saw it as, "a close one." Years later I came not to the belief, but to the knowledge that God's Face emerged. He was in the midst. I met Destiny – a spirit, who always reminds me in conversation that I am to understand and remember the lessons learned.

Destiny snuck into the room where I slept that random night at the winter cabin. When I opened my eyes, I saw her force which seemed different in the darkness. Destiny has no skin or pigment because she is a spirit so initially, I was afraid. I noticed when I quick-right-hook-punched downward to the floor to shoo her away, she stepped back just a little bit for me to relax. When I looked across the room and over the open floor, there were two light beings resembling human fraternal twins, a boy, and a girl. Their legs were swinging playfully in tandem as they waved hello. I was not hallucinating; I knew what I saw and maintain I did not go crazy.

I whispered to Erik, who slept soundly in the bunk above mine. I was freaking out much more dramatically than the little boy from the movie, *"The Sixth Sense,"* because *"I see light people."*

I screamed to the top of my lungs. The lights came on and of course I am looking like a hot mess suddenly speaking a slurred-drunken-Danish I suppose. I was frantic and incapable of really expressing that I was scared out of my mind. My Swedish was limited and the same applied for the others in the room since their English was limited, too. I was advised to chuck it down as a nightmare eyes wide shut by Margareta, Erik's mother, as Ragnar, Margareta's husband and daughter, Brita, looked on.

Ironically, as the hands of the clock moved forward as with the flow of time, I was about to go to sleep in my bedroom at the Counselor's house. There is nothing extraordinary because by now I had lived there for weeks. I turned my light off feeling sleepy. At some point I was awake struggling to get up because I felt like I was in the middle of a windy storm. The wind was strong, too. I could not get up no matter how hard I tried, and I was so afraid. After some time, the wind stopped and the lamp I knew I turned off by habit was on. I did not find it very strange, but part of me wondered how it got on. The following morning as I ate breakfast before heading to school, I spoke as I normally did to my Counselor's wife, Margareta.

She began to recount a dream before I politely interrupted to ask her the brief question, "Did you turn on my lamp last night, Margareta"? "No", she said. "But I had the strangest dream last night. I never dream about my mother. She has been dead for many years now. She approached me in the dream and told me to turn on the light because Angelo is afraid of the dark." A chill crept down my spine.

Could this be another Face of God? Was it a coincidence? It could be. If God be the Creator and everything in it, seen and unseen, could we deny that He is powerful enough to show His face unconventionally? He is Spirit.

What is more is that many homes in Sweden are generational and when you visit, the bitterly cold weather promotes a chilling atmosphere most of the time. As sure as there are wild fields, mountains, valleys and plains, there is the strong possibility that spirits roam in a realm unseen. God and His hosts cannot be placed in one tightly packaged box. When you have undeniable encounters with the Source, you could never fully be the same.

My year in Sweden brought fond memories. The crowning moment was a three-week tour throughout Europe at the end of the exchange year. The trip afforded me the opportunity to see countries like Denmark, Germany, Belgium, The Netherlands, France, Italy, Czech

Republic, and Austria. The memories are unforgettable and will have left an indescribable imprint on my heart.

Most life-changing, even more now, is the knowledge that when I was alone dancing through countries an ocean away, the Creator was there. Take a moment to think about what is being declared. I was a world away and the people who I grew up knowing physically were not.

The God of Many Faces, however, showed up. Sometimes He appeared invisibly and mysteriously. At other times He manifested through the faces I came to behold as we interacted through that passage of time. The few examples I shared are simply that – a few.

I am certain that there are many people in the world who have had fascinating encounters with the Most-High and His hosts. Such talks are culturally considered taboo and attach stigma on people who share these experiences. To many persons, my examples only touch the surface in comparison to far more profound ones with the divine. It does not matter the depth, really, but rather the willingness to venture into the deeper truth of God.

CHAPTER THREE
God Emerged

Like the still of the night, dusk had turned pitch-black, and as dawn approached to the summons of the sunlight, I was left feeling bittersweet. I felt a type of so-so because my exchange year was finally ending. It was an adventure I knew I soon would not forget. It was a journey – such an unforgettable one, which afforded me the opportunity to meet people from many walks of life. By then I was living with my fifth host family. Earlier I mentioned walking into a pack of wolves. Shortly after that incident, I left my first host family.

My second host family will have been my Counselor, his wife, and her father, Lars, or "Lasse." He was quite a laugh because his laugh was a laugh non-stop. The mansion in which I resided for about a month sometimes made me feel like Lasse did not reside there. He lived on the other side of the rather large place. The only time that I saw Lasse is on those random occasions when I took a shower by his bedroom or in passing to do my laundry.

Then I moved in with a Philosophy Teacher and his wife, who both worked at the school I attended. They had two daughters. My fourth home was very unique; my host father, host mother, and host siblings, lived the "Alternative Life" translated from Swedish to English. And no, it did not involve homosexuality in case you are thinking it. It simply means that they lived in a way to protect the Earth. They used and ate environmentally friendly "everything" and grew and bought food that is organic.

    I enjoyed living with them, but it lasted for a very short while because I resided far from school. Just walking from home to the bus stop was a challenge. I was then accommodated by the fifth and last host family. My host dad owned a construction company, my host mother was a Principal and they had two teenage daughters who I met at school. Each household was memorable in different ways, so my host families are held in a very special place in my heart.

    Imagine me in a fully loaded apartment. Indeed, I was spoiled and loved every bit of it. My final family was equally as loving and caring as all the rest, but I was super fortunate to be housed in their vacant apartment that was attached to the front of their home. The story of how I got to live there was that I befriended a student who would become my eldest host sister. One day I had arrived at school and thus, confided in her that I had been living in a home far into the forest. I merely mentioned that it would have been easier for me to get to school had I lived somewhere closer. It was the reason she approached her parents. It was a go. They welcomed me to their home for the shortest period during my exchange year. However, as I marked the calendar to my return home, it was at the same apartment where I would become most overwhelmed. I had to accept leaving the many friends I made, hold onto the memories which slowly fade, and depart a country that became home. I began to receive presents and the best of wishes in cards bearing, "goodbye."

It was not as simple for me as packing and boarding a flight to return home. There were heavy responsibilities that arose for being such a warm human. I was selected of the three exchange students that year to speak on behalf of us all at our high school graduation ceremony because I was most fluent in the language. Of course, I was excited, but not really interested in all that was required to prepare. I wrote my speech with the help of my host sisters for certain words and phrases that sounded more "native" than "migrant." It was great to have delivered that speech and receive a resounding applause.

It took me back to the camp where I learned the basics – the camp that I feared would no longer be afforded to me because of losing the course money needed to benefit from the learning experience. I was amazed at the God of Second Chances – that forgiving God. I could see Him smiling in the audience as He cheered me on through the many familiar and unfamiliar faces.

The next hurdle was my having to pack – not once, but twice. I had accumulated so much during that period and was due to go on a tour of Europe for three weeks. So it was difficult to shed the extra from what was not so extra. I had to separate what I knew I was going to take with me on the flight back to The Bahamas from what I needed to leave behind. I had to consider that two pieces of luggage and a carry – on was insufficient space to carry my whole kit and caboodle. I took issue with that. How dare the airline not understand that I had been upgraded to a "worldwide traveler" and was bound to buy a trinket in every destination! I had to come up with a strategy and so I decided that I would only carry with me what was very necessary on the European tour.

However, I left behind packed belongings that could be adjusted after the tour was complete. It just seemed more progressive to keep things organized so that when I got back, if I needed to rest from all the excitement, I would not be burdened by getting myself together last-minute.

In the blink of an eye, it was like I was teleported to the future. I sat on a bus with exchange students I met and was pleased to be introduced to new ones. They would be my companions for three weeks. It was so fun. Every time we got on the bus from town to town and country to country, Zifa's song, "On the Road Again" could be heard. Zifa is a popular Swedish Artist who lived in South Africa for a part of his life. His music incorporated some very intriguing sounds that were clearly from the Motherland.

I remember the highlights of the trip like it was yesterday. It started on the bridge from Sweden to Denmark; t'was such an awakening to realize that Europe is beyond beautiful – so pristine and inviting. I remember exploring the ferry onto which the bus drove from Denmark en route to Germany. This was after two African janitors in some public Danish bathroom stole my thumb rings and chose to be dumb when asked that they return them. When they denied stealing the rings, I turned blue-mad just as those women were black as tar to turn mad-blue in the moonlight!

At some point the bus drove onward into the mountains of Lüdenscheid, Germany. That is where I ate my first, very-beefy Beef Stroganoff and tried a schnitzel in a Kaiser bun. I could remember the Berlin Wall, but I was more fascinated about their taxis being Mercedes Benz; that I arrived in a destination where the brand is not so luxurious, but "like so normal."

I remember Belgium and the odd hotel selected for our stay, the famous Manneken Pis and the Good Luck Leper in Brussels. Yet, my mind was captured by the taste of assorted white Belgian chocolates – heaven.

I remembered visiting Austria, and despite my teardrops at Auschwitz, where many Jews were killed by Hitler, *"the hills did thrill my heart and resound in music."* The bus drove through Salzburg where the actual Von Trapp family lived whose stories inspired the movie, *"The Sound of Music."*

I remember Prague and thinking that a vampire must be around the bend because the level of gothic was surreal. I remember France – the tasty pastries and the lights at Moulin Rouge. I remember Italy – my crispy, all-for-me, thin-crust pizza before a romantic gondola ride in Venice. The city is actually sinking just as the sand in an hourglass. Time was again running out too fast.

Three weeks passed like a gentle wind. I could see myself sitting on that final train ride to Sweden's Airport, Stockholm Arlanda. It was so painful watching my host mother, Inger, wave goodbye as her face grew sullen and blush-red. My subtle tears wanted to flow more violently, but they receded every time I thought of how badly I wanted to reunite with my own family. I was now accustomed to travelling a lot.

    Swedish was not sounding so funny anymore, but the newfound comedy was how my English changed. I was somehow speaking my native language a bit in reverse. For example, I would say, "Can I be getting some water, thank you" as opposed to, "may I have some water please." That was a simple change. There were even stranger statements that I would make because that is how my brain worked. I was able to learn Swedish because my brain wired itself according to sentence structure and not so much on a literal translation. The seat on the train became the seat on the plane. I was finally airborne.

    Beyond nine hours later, I was flying over Miami. There is something about the tropics. For those who have had the privilege of travelling on a transatlantic flight to and from destinations as I did, can confirm this truth. When you fly to Europe, there is an unveiling of God's majesty through green, white and blue. Upon return to the tropics there is an unveiling of God's majesty through blues – plural. The shades of blues range from midnight, near black, to turquoise and sky blue that seem cooling and crystal clear. To have seen the view from the sky after a long year, however memorable, was a kiss from heaven.

    I was eager to deplane. I knew that my mother would be waiting alone at the airport for me because daddy was too busy with work. Mommy told he was not coming but assured me that he was super-happy to hear that I was on my way home. I finally arrived in the open arrivals area where people picked up their loved ones. I had an image stored in my mind of how mommy should look so I was focused anxiously for the woman with whom I spent most of my life outside the walls of a traditional school.

She waved at me. I could tell her voice. I glimpsed this woman before, but I had not recognized her. I could not recognize her just as I could not believe she chose to wear those huge spaceship-looking glasses. I flinch as I think about it. It totally shattered the view of the woman I remembered.

It was equally confusing for mommy who remembered my departure with a low haircut – near bald with slight waves. She would come to meet a young man with a fairer complexion and afro-buds popping on my scalp like a break-out of measles. I thought it was cool. I am sure it was "different" and as strange as I must have been to choose such a weird look. Mommy looked at it and chuckled.

I remembered her asking me what happened to my hair. I told her I wanted to try something different. She encouraged me to be different but was convinced that it should be properly done. I am sure she was silently mortified. In a rental car, we left.

That night we sat at Bennigan's, a restaurant near the hotel at which mommy and I would stay a few nights before returning home to Freeport, Grand Bahama. It is an island located in The Bahamas and nestled north within the Bahama archipelago. The reunion was lovely.

Upon arrival in Grand Bahama, daddy went all out. He clearly missed me. A limousine was rented for the ride from the airport to our house. A lot had changed in a year. Perhaps a lot did not change, but combined with my memories of Europe, no matter how small the change it will have appeared to be big. I felt so happy and welcome. It was good to breathe the salt of the air and even nicer to feel the gentle, Bahamian breeze. I knew I was home when the heat of the sun felt hot as a furnace. It was August 2001.

Finally, home – I was a two-time High School graduate. Who does that? It is bizarre. To many it would be grander to hold a double major at a degree level and even up to the Doctorate Degree. Yet, my question is how many High School graduates have experienced the "Swedish" sailor-like cap being worn only to be collectively thrown in the air having just graduated?

How many High school students will have learned a foreign language fluently? How many High School students will have vacationed to so many destinations during their secondary studies? How many High School students are forced to avoid ethnocentrism; the belief that one's culture is better than another?

I would question as far up to the holder of the Doctorate Degree. Indeed, there are those who have experienced amazing journeys especially if their university courses required that much. But I am sure the in-depth celebration of another culture is an adventure taken by a vast minority of persons.

I returned to The Bahamas shortly before the bombing of the World Trade Center in New York City. When many people were perhaps afraid of Muslims or perhaps scorned them, I was not so quick to engage this attitude as young as I was because I could grasp that all Muslims are not terrorists. I discussed, debated, laughed, and played in their homes. They were the pure Muslims who were as loving and open as I am. They were hospitable to me. The only difference, most of the times, was my race and religion.

Those terrorists in the 2001 bombing could not be the same kind of people I had the honor of knowing. Genuine Muslims represent the reverence and discipline of Allah – a stricter Face of the Universal God. Terrorists do not wear a face of the Creator; they wear the Mask of Evil and Murderous Agenda – it is that simple. Any extremist, fundamentalist or terrorist-bawl-out murderers who kill in the name of the Most-High are evil, and do not resemble the Face of God.

Progressively, I was due to start College in January 2002. Because I had arrived home in August, it will have been a bit of a rush to start in the autumn. Too, it will have given me sufficient time to get my sentences together seeing that I was speaking a type of mumbo-jumbo.

Mommy came through on her promise. Looking back at it I am now convinced mommy did not want to hurt my feelings. She was so determined to tidy up my afro-budded hairstyle that she looked for a well-known hair braider in the ghetto. This hair braider was considered an expert because she could braid *"picky hair"* or *"peasy hair."* Bahamians are having a laugh because we refer to black people with rough-textured hair as *"peasy-headed."* It is no term of endearment for the lovelies – it is reserved for the people who were blessed with hair not so easy to brush or comb.

I was a bit baffled by my mother's guarantee that my hair could be braided. And the day came when I would sit down and let the braiding lady align corn row plaits from my hairline at the top of my forehead down to the back of my neck. As she pulled my strands, I could feel my hair tighten – scream even. I could feel the pinch as my face lifted.

When it was all over, I was handed a mirror and my reflection was one of shock horror. The saddening thing is I was not controlling it. Indeed, I was shocked that the braiding lady managed to braid my hair but imagine expressing shock and it was against your will. Even if I wanted to confess that I did not like the style, the expressed shock on my face would have made the braider feel otherwise. My eyebrows were magically lifted, and my eyelashes were forced to follow suit. Imagine that.

From young I wanted to be an Attorney. After befriending my Eritrean friend-girl who told me of her touching story, I was stimulated all the more. It was the injustice and the breach of Human Rights that spoke to my soul. It was the fact that many people could speak out in their minds, but it impacted as a whisper in the real world. Soon I would study Pre-Law at a College in the Capital.

At the time, my only brother recently had his first child, Triston. I used to call my newly-born nephew, "the pink thing." He was so pink with a grade of silky black hair. I would soon be relocating to Nassau to live with my brother and Triston's mother, Kelly. Life was beginning to become grounded. For one year I lived a type of fantasy. I existed in some dream world because it was a chance in life that most will never say they have had the pleasure of having. It is the way it is and precisely the way it was.

There is a clear difference between Freeport, Grand Bahama and Nassau, New Providence. Where I was born, people are known to be very reserved. It is a city where people are friendly, but do not necessarily know their neighbors. If you are remotely social, you might recognize them from time to time to say a cordial "hello" or wave in acknowledgement. I am not saying that this is the same for everybody in Grand Bahama. There are the townships where communities are in fact communities and neighbors will be neighbors. They tend to be the friendlier country folk from the extreme East or West of the island where villages called *"settlements"* are mainly built by generations of families who are known to be most hospitable. And with that said, you would want to avoid having the slightest grudge with any resident since that person is likely to be related to someone a stone-throw away. That spells conflict.

But I am a Freeport-city guy. Indeed, we are just as candy-mannerly as the Negroes of the south in the United

States. We will chit-chat and smile maintaining an acceptable distance. You will feel the warmly-standoffishness like "island elite." When we travel within the country, somehow, we stand out. We look no different – but to other Bahamians we act *"sophisticated"* and *"stuck up."*

You see in Nassau, even if Bahamians wanted to maintain an air of being "standoffish" they could not because of traffic congestion, close-enough housing, and the obvious day-to-day routine. The Nassau-Islander called *"Nassauvian"* (Nass-Sue-vee-un) represents the true city-trained citizen. They are more aggressive, bold and go-get-em'. They are louder but more unified.

Neighbors are bound to know their neighbors unless communities have become doomed by private people. Impossible – Nassau is too small! The Bahamas is more Nassau-centric because Nassau, being the capital, remains the heart of the nation's economy. To a tourist, the island is a snap-photo from a postcard. To average Bahamians, there are beautiful areas to behold in Nassau, but the island is dirty to us.

Compared to the outer islands, that we call, *"Family Islands"*, Nassau's nature has been polluted. Remember, The Bahamas is made up of 700 islands to explore and its majesty generally remains untouched as a virgin. I travelled to Nassau countless times throughout my childhood, so I was quite ready to embrace change as far as my college career.

College was going very well, and I made new friends with whom I am still in touch today. There were the best of times and the worst of times. I can say that the best of times surely outweighed the worst of times. With time we learn many lessons. There were the best of lessons and the worst of lessons. It is said that what does not kill you only makes you stronger.

Living with my big brother, Darmeeko, having mutually matured a bit, exposed me to another side of him. I was able to experience his more relaxed side, but an entirely beastly side, too. I was no longer the little baby brother who needed big-brother protection. Instead, he became a role model to a younger brother who should know better. With that change there were times we laughed until we could not breathe. At other times we argued to the point that if I did not back off, I am sure my teeth will have gone missing. I love him so much. I hated him, too. Yet, in the end, I realized just how much I truly love him because he was and will always be my big brother. He is always there for me. Until this day we are still close. We might not speak to each other every day, but we keep in touch sufficiently. We know we have got each other and that is what is most important.

One must bear in mind that Europe took a toll on me. I was no longer island-innocent. I learned to party into the midnight. I learned to be smashed for a change. I learned how to breathe a good smoke of tobacco-sweet air. I liked Salem. I liked the cooling chill of menthol damaging my lungs. I remember that evening I lost innocence like a nervous virgin girl who was about to experience her first *"big one."*

My New Zealander friend with his rebellious, British-hybrid accent was the culprit – yes, his scalawag twang sounded like a British sailor with a loose tongue. He was petrified at the thought that I could be so sane without a drop of alcohol. He insisted that I must pop my cherry, and so the daredevil would encourage that we go easy with something light. I will never forget my first drink. It was a Baileys, Kailua, and milk.

I took my first sip and choked from what tasted like fluid candy. I knew it was sin, but I developed an appetite for it. I refuse to lie. I enjoyed the variety of drink and the degrees of buzz I felt on the dance floor. I have no regrets – just great memories of what it felt like to be young and carefree.

In Nassau, Darmeeko, called "Meeko" for short, realized that Europe changed me. I was so worldly, but not entirely corrupted. I just loved to party. Being my older sibling, Meeko was awesome in that he was not controlling or "un-cool." He was able to give guidance and encourage me to make better choices. The fact that Meeko is a University graduate made him appreciate my drive to reach the balance of enjoying the nightlife and achieving good grades.

I was able to pull it off, but how I miss the ability to remember a lot of information. I actually loved learning back then but could not imagine going back to university study. I will not say I am opposed to the idea, but I am not sure that I would enjoy the experience as much as I did during my younger years.

There are certainly highlights that come to mind when I think of my College years in Nassau. I remember when Meeko, his girlfriend, my nephew and I lived at that bright pink set of apartments on that main thoroughfare on the way to College. It was a busy highway. I liked living there although the color of my environment made me feel like I lived among pink flamingoes. Every time I sat on the toilet at those apartments to take a good shit, the girlfriend next door seemed to be thrown into the wall. It was clockwork. The timing made me feel like the sniff of my fart made the boyfriend angry. For some reason, their fights were more comical and not necessarily an appeal to report domestic violence or abuse. The girlfriend was sassy and sometimes she could be heard picking a fuss for a perhaps balanced level of aggression in that relationship. Indeed, it led to loud, make-up sex.

Armageddon had finally come. I was home completing a class assignment and Meeko was upstairs watching television. All of a sudden, I heard the girlfriend yelling and she was very angry. She called out to her "bae-come-whoop-me." I went upstairs to my room to see what was happening a bit more clearly. As I looked out of my bedroom window, I saw "Boo-thang" climbing out of his bedroom window barely dressed. He was in escape mode. He managed to put on his clothes with the quickness of a runway model about to hit the catwalk. I witnessed that man jump off the roof like a mischievous monkey, get into his car and speed off like a pit-bull-dog was chasing him. I could not figure out fully what was going on.

As I listened, I could hear the angry girlfriend firing words of profanity, commanding that whoever was in the apartment, "open up the fucking door before she broke it open!" Meeko saw me in a daze and asked what was wrong as I explained what I witnessed.

We went downstairs and then outside where we saw the girlfriend talking to the front door of her apartment. I was convinced she would need a stray jacket. Her anger seemed demonic. She started kicking the door determined that by some superpower she could *"bionic woman"* the door down. But what was most unexpected was the soft, apologetic voice behind the door pleading that she will open the door if the girlfriend would please calm down and not kill her. The more the lady spoke, the angrier the girlfriend became. As I listened, I could hear a faint, frightened Jamaican accent, *"Me-say please-meez, me-ah-oh-pain-neet."*

I knew what was happening now. Young Jamaican women in this dilemma had and still have a poor reputation for breaking up Bahamian homes.

Darmeeko found this event to be an ideal opportunity to provide popcorn he managed to pop in the microwave – literally. Believe me he popped a bowl because it was a scene from the year's best thriller. All of a sudden, the girlfriend made one final appeal addressing the apparent slut behind the door, *"seeing that you do not want to open the door after I asked you kindly, I will show you how unkind I could be."* She stormed away and the crowd that gathered followed behind her to the rear of the apartment as though we were protestors for justice. It became *"fright-night"* the moment she chose to take out a large-ass butcher knife.

Unveiling a gymnast, the girlfriend climbed the wall onto the roof like Spiderman up to the bedroom window and busted the window into the apartment. The crowd in turn had a psychic moment and the collective bingo ran the entire crowd screaming to the front door. The person arriving first started to slam-knock the door to get the girlfriend to open it. It was not long after the appeal that we began to hear things crashing inside as the girl screamed for her dear life. The door began to open as if it were being unlocked by a ghost.

Opening the door like the new heroine on the block, the girlfriend invited the entire crowd into the apartment where apparent slackness unfolded. She then proceeded to provide a grand tour of the apartment drawing our attention to a used tampon in the upstairs toilet. I gagged. As she brought the tour to a close, the more furious she became. Meanwhile, the prostitute was forcibly commanded to sit down and shut up. She dared not move because all she saw was the end of her life.

The shamed woman would be thrown out of the apartment screaming what appeared to be the most broken form of Jamaican Patois I had ever heard. It must have been fear. The girlfriend fake-attempted to stab the accused to increase her fear and eventually freed her with the threat that if the prostitute were ever seen close to her man she would be diced like tomatoes. To this day I have not fully grasped the magic that caused the loose woman to run desperately for her life. As shocked as I was, I managed to help Meeko eat the popcorn.

Many incidents played out – too many to relate. There were the triumphant times and there were times I would fail. I endured until the day I received my Associates Degree. I had accomplished another milestone and was so grateful to have remained focus to a victorious end. But the journey would not end there. I was once again on my way to Europe. This time it was not to be an exchange student. I was headed to fulfill my dream of being an Attorney. It would require three years. The day had finally come that Nassau also became too small. When I say too small, I am not saying that Nassau is any less beautiful even to date, but I could feel that my time there was divinely set to close. There was a summons to a higher calling that I would come to know to be completely different from any accomplishment that I will have ever expected.

Hurricane Frances devastated Freeport shortly after I moved back home in 2004 on my way to law school. It was a terrible experience. I remember in the midst of the storm thinking aloud that only the grace of the Creator could spare my life. Interestingly, I was booked with British Airways to fly from Freeport to Miami and Miami onto London Heathrow. After the hurricane, it became clear that the original route could not happen. The reality, too, is that when a hurricane affects the Bahamas, every island of the Bahama chain is not impacted. Flights from Nassau remained on schedule.

School was due to start September 2004, and the concern was whether or not flights could resume from Freeport on time since the airport had been severely damaged. Miraculously, the airport was fit for flights to resume on time, but only domestic ones. Thus, I was re-routed to Nassau where I stayed with my brother for a few days and then onto Miami where I would catch the originating flight from there to London.

It was happening all too fast, but it happened most importantly. The meal I ate the evening before was a Bahamian treat that I know I would not taste for a while. I absolutely devoured a mean cracked conch and fries with ketchup and hot sauce courtesy of big brother. I was so content because in the morning I was off to University. Jolly, good ole' England, here I come!

I managed to finally make it to my seat on British Airways having endured a short 45-minute flight from Nassau to Miami. I then got my bags at the baggage claim in Miami, and proceeded to the gate, on time, post check-in. I do not recall a very long wait before being welcomed aboard.

British Airways was quite the experience. I can remember laughing at the safety demonstrations in such polished English. It was not like I was travelling to England for the first time. During my exchange year in Sweden, the Rotary Club treated each student under scholarship to a trip abroad and a domestic ski trip. That year, England was the destination of choice. The club would pay for accommodations and airfare. Parents would be responsible for food and spending money.

I could remember travelling to London with other exchange students. We were not really strangers because most of us met before. The new faces might have been exchange students from Australia because their program usually started at the end of January of a given exchange year.

It was quite the encounter that evening to be walking with companions and chaperones to have seen a woman in the distance. As we got closer, we could see that the woman was clothed in a fitted black leather cat suit with robust, pink feathers. Her face was well painted with powder, eyeliner, and rather colorful lipstick. She was a prostitute – a London hustler of the night. I was so taken back by her bold appeal to exchange sex for money. She was *"dead-set"* on that Pound Sterling! Unfortunately, no one from our group was even slightly interested or rich enough to fulfill her advances – poor woman.

The flicker of flashbacks was occupying my mind, as I patiently waited for the huge aircraft to be filled by passengers. Apparently, the flight was booked to capacity – a 747 jumbo jet with upstairs, downstairs and five seating classes. I was so economy – so student. I did not mind. To return to England was luxurious enough. The opportunity was luxurious enough – well, accomplished enough. The time came when the wait would be over.

The airplane began to reverse, and then taxi in the direction of the runway for what took an eternity. Every unevenness and bump of the tarmac was felt and the upstairs cabin seemed like it was shifting from left to right. Drops on the ride toward the runway were heavy and gravity-fallen.

It took very long for the airplane to lift off the ground. The gravity grew extremely intense and it was at that point I realized we were airborne. The feeling of being bully-planted to my seat finally subsided the moment the aircraft leveled high in the sky. The captain welcomed everyone aboard and informed us that the voyage would be some eight hours and thirty minutes.

It must have been a smooth flight. I drifted to sleep for the most part. I had finally arrived in London Heathrow, but not my luggage. For those who have had to endure those long walks to the baggage claim can understand why I felt extremely agitated at the airport.

During my on-boarding process for University as an international student, my pick-up, one-way, was arranged to the campus, courtesy of the University. I was pleasantly greeted by a young, black British student who oversaw student affairs. He was the right person for the position because he was thorough and engaging. As we got to know each other, he shared that the majority of his family migrated from Jamaica. He had a unique sound – the gab of the Southern Londoner. It rang of an urban swag.

I eventually would disclose that I needed assistance with retrieving my baggage that somehow got lost in transit. My first pal at the university was able to connect with British Airways and I was put on the telephone with the department responsible for lost bags. I had the task of having to describe how the bags looked, among other things, so that the airline could initiate the search for what could have wound up anywhere. I was told that I will have to return a call in a few days for a result and discussions would continue about compensation.

There I was with no real change of clothing during Fresher's Week. Fresher's week is like orientation week within more westernized academic institutions. There is a very refined approach in England – a type of wine and cheese affair and a mini smörgåsbord to be enjoyed here and there. Also, there were many events scheduled at which I wanted to participate. However, I was stuck with one outfit – the same outfit I wore on my arrival to law school.

I will never forget it. I wore some non-designer-brand t-shirt, a mustard yellow Ralph Lauren pullover a cousin bought me one lucky Christmas and blue denim jeans. I made the best of the experience because you are only a Fresher once. I was brave enough to meet and greet the hundreds of students who were just as interesting as me to have a laugh. If I were looking to be popular, I would certainly be known because the mustard-yellow pullover illuminated my proudly strutting torso. I was not fashioned to ever be a small person but a thick, beefy young man.

Days later I returned a call to British Airways. Up until then I was becoming used to the new environment and familiar with the students assigned to rooms on my corridor. That is another thing that might be a bit different schooling in England.

Accommodations, especially at my University of choice, were a bit "posh." A corridor is like a hallway of rooms where one student is assigned per room. Nonetheless, there was only one communal shower and a bathroom that housed a tub for baths. Corridors were available to students in each college. A University then is not usually a main building, but a collection of colleges. Freshers tend to reside in those single-occupant dorm rooms for the first year and then move to on-campus housing or housing off campus.

I recall those fun conversations on my corridor with newfound friends. There was one in particular; one that taught me the word, *"trousers."* My new, white friends turned beet-red when I asserted, "I really need some new *"pants."* To them I must *"have fancied wearing knickers"* which is the same as wearing female underwear. It was the same shock horror I endured when a guy from Essex excused himself mid-conversation and said, *"I'll be back; gonna' light a fag"* as if some innocent gay was about to die. Eventually, I learned that a *"fag,"* is a cigarette also known as a *"ciggy."* Despite these comically-embarrassing developments I am thankful for the extra change my parents provided to buy underclothing until my baggage could be retrieved.

I vaguely recall the conversation with British Airways. I truly appreciated their service – even now. I was offered compensation for the inconvenience that doubled in amount when I appealed most sassy-forward that my Fresher's week was not so refreshing because of their negligence. The phone would eventually hang up. I felt satisfied. Days went by. I received my compensation. Finally, law school was beginning to feel a lot more like I had plunged into an ocean of possibility.

I began to sway with the rhythm of University life. It was a newfound path of profound lectures I was determined not to confound me. It was the start of a budding relationship with the library that would caress me into the wee-wee hours of the morning. For once I would surrender to the reality that partying every so often was required to maintain peace of mind. I can see myself for endless hours looking pensively at my inflated law books and thinking that the authors both had no life outside genius and must have been cold blooded. Somehow, I enjoyed learning and managed to spill my thoughts onto paper and meet my deadlines with some research on the subject matter. I took the good with the bad. I got good grades. I got bad grades. I got graded between – a grade that degrades to another that upgrades. It was the power of prevailing that mattered, and I was faring well.

I am now twenty-three years of age and it was the second year into my law course. I was headed to my campus apartment on a path not uncommonly taken. The weather was cool, yet the sun was shining. There was a gentle breeze that made the tree leaves quiver. I was walking and could feel a presence. Spirit was there, but quite invisible. I knew it was an encounter, but my words could not paint the feeling. I did not feel fear, but I felt a chilly-warm embrace. Just perhaps I was lost in what can be described as *"spiritual shock."* It was like the thrill a crazed person feels when surprised by a celebrity, but the adrenaline refuses to subside. It bubbled over.

As I walked into what seemed like an enhanced vision, I could hear a voice, *"I am the trees, I am the birds; can't you hear me in the wind? I am the sun, the rain, and everything that is – I am."* As I heard the voice, my senses could feel what was being said. My environment actually provided the experience. I saw the leaves of trees dance. I saw the birds fly and swoon. The sun seemed to get hotter yet suddenly it started to drizzle like each word was commanded to happen.

To this day I know that I had not been drinking or partying the night before. I am certain that it was midweek because I can vividly recall that I was wearing my backpack headed home after class. It was very rare that I would go to a club during the week or even be under the influence at that time of the day. If I drank, and of course my favorite was dry, white wine, I would usually sip slowly as I read those thick law books to keep myself calm. I did not smoke cannabis or tobacco, nor did I ever contemplate any strong drug. My mind was not being altered by some substance that I used or abused. I came to the realization many years later that this awesome encounter would be the prelude of revelations that would be much more enlightening. I have learned that one must brace in grace for a clearer Face of God.

CHAPTER FOUR
Simply Profound

There is no word known to man in our universal vocabulary that can define the Creator. He is indescribable; He is invisible; a spiritual presence that is here, there and everywhere. The thing about the unseen world is that it is very hard to believe it exists because we cannot readily see it. Interestingly, I believe that the Creator knew that His existence would be challenged, and that humans would attempt to forget Him and all the credit that He deserves.

In the simplicity of life, however, if we dare remove the mental blocks that we hold very strong in our minds, we will find the simple answer. We can ask ourselves questions that make the truth very loud and clear. For example, when you ask the question, *"can I create a tree,"* the answer will be no. Even if scientists attempt to fool the masses and copy every tree known to man, challenge them to create a seed of a tree that does not exist. It is impossible. Who created the seed then?

Renowned Gospel Singer Nicole C. Mullen declared in the song, *"My Redeemer Lives"* some major questions:

- Who is responsible for the sunrise?
- Who is responsible for the churn of waves to their hidden boundaries?
- Who is responsible for the sunset to the summons of the invisible moon?
- Whose command reverberates and the world bows?

- Who is responsible for the orbit?
- Who is this God of Many Faces so powerful yet gentle in one?
- Who is this marvelous Giver of Life over Death?

Through additional readings, I discovered some disciplined words of "Salah" that Muslims use when they pray translated to English:

> "There is nothing but you,
> Every great scholar is your student,
> In every scent, there is nothing but you,
>
> Creator of and worshipped by both worlds,
> Everything is witness to your manifestation,
> On everyone's lips is your prayer,
>
> In every chord, every song is your presence,
> Every beginning is with your name,
> With your name ends everything,
>
> Your praise is 'praise be to Allah',
> That you are the God of my Mohammad,
> When this Earth and world did not exist,
>
> When there was no moon, sun, or sky,
> When the secret of the truth was still unknown,
> When there was nothing, there was you,

Everything is a reflection of your glory.
Everything cries out that you are the Lord,
It is the distinction of your enthralling visage,

You are the unrivalled Lord of the Universe,
You who shows new beauty every instant,
Surprises even those who yearn for more,

Every sapling sings of your creation,
Every leaf is a signature of your nature,
My God, you are the splendor you promised,

You are the curiosity, you are the desire,
The light of my eyes, the voice of my heart,
You were, you are, and will be only you,

You are everything, what is the argument in this,
The whole world is searching only for you,
Even as your magnificence is in every corner,
You are in my blood, Lord of the world."

And lastly, consider some words of, *"Om Jai Jagdish"*, the universal prayer or *"aarti"* of Hinduism that speaks to the nature of God or *"Brahma."* It is translated to English:

"Oh Lord of the Universe,
Thou art my mother and father,
Thou art the ancient great soul,

Lord, thou art the omnipotent master,
Perfect, Absolute, Supreme God,
Thou art the Lord of everything and everyone,

Thou art an ocean of mercy,
Lord, thou art the protector,
I am a simpleton with vain desires,

I am a servant and thou art the Lord,
Oh Lord, grant me thy divine grace,
Oh Lord of the Universe,

You are the one unseen,
Of all living beings,
The Lord of all living beings,
Grant me a glimpse,
Guide me along the path to thee,
Oh Lord of the Universe,

Friend of the helpless and feeble,
Lord, you are my noble,
Lift up your hand,
Offer me thy refuge,
At thy feet,
Oh Lord of the Universe,

Remove the corruption of the mind,
Defeat evil, Supreme Soul,
Lord, defeat evil,
Grow my faith and devotion,
Oh Lord, grow my faith and devotion,
So I may serve the saints,
Oh Lord of the Universe."

When comparing those rather poetic words across three religions, I sense that collectively we are praying to one Universal Creator. The way I praise as a Christian is no more correct than a Muslim or Hindu that prays to who I call Jehovah God. Their way is not wrong, and they are not damned, to the proverbial Christian hell, nor is my way incorrect either. We simply worship differently; that is all to it.

On my spiritual journey more recently, this thought has been very much supported by a vision I experienced years ago when I resided in England. It is said that hindsight is 20/20 and now in 2020, this book is being written to share a very possible truth. And the truth is on our spiritual journeys, we are not to tear down what we know, but simply to explore outside of religious boundaries to further strengthen our faith. This research can only make us more aware and not necessarily destroy individual faith. In other words, it cannot be the case that a person who is secure in one religion is more secure than a person who has ventured to compare others to maintain a certain belief. Faith and conviction make an idea concrete to us, but it is not as concrete as basing that conviction on a spiritually-guided comparison of other religious theories.

If a believer is persuaded to convert to another belief, there was no real agreement initially. Spiritual awakening should be liberal. Children born into any religion or non-religion, for example, can be taught the basis of faith, but equally be encouraged to search for themselves when they are old enough to do so. Again, the Creator has many faces.

There I am on that normal day at law school with two female, Hindu friends. They were sisters from Kenya. The upcoming Moot was very strong on our minds. Moots are simply debate competitions in British law schools. My mooting partner was a Hindu friend of mine. That day he was not around but his girlfriend, her sister and I wound up discussing the moot. Somehow, I forgot that I needed a white dress shirt to appear before the Law Lords at the moot. We made an immediate decision to go on a hunt for one. Canterbury-English prices are expensive if you do not know where to go for the savings. This time round the deal was available at British Home Stores. The white dress shirt came with a tie and was all I needed. I was set for the competition.

If I am recalling correctly, my friend and I competed against two young ladies from Africa. We lost overall because Moots are actually designed that way. Due to the way law operates, there can only be one right decision. A young Nigerian lady would be the top debater that evening because she truly presented very strong arguments.

After the moot that evening, there was a little after-party held where all competitors could formally meet the Law Lords. I do remember I was asked the question, what do you want to become after Law School by the seemingly most curious of them. My answer was, "I want to be a great ruler of my nation." I am unsure if the wine made me blurt out this poetry, but I do recall the Law Lords looking at each other with mysterious reaction.

I asked my friend and worthy mooting partner what he thought about that answer. He responded that he found it declaratory so just perhaps I had a strong conviction to be a trailblazer even though I did not become an Attorney per se. The Law Lords simply chimed in, *"Here, here"* encouraging me to do my best. I will never forget that occasion for the rest of my life – such a powerful panel of invited guests from the House of Lords, London.

Later that evening, I knew that I was in a coherent place. I never drank too much. If I ever went over the normal amount there was a temporary buzz of absolute bliss for a fleeting moment, but I was quite calm in my mind. However, I felt tired. Escorting me home was a good friend from Pakistan, Aleem, who called me on my mobile phone to congratulate me since I expressed a disinterest in the moot weeks prior. He asked if we could meet up. We hung out together as we walked breathing in the fresh night air. Time went too quickly so we would part ways. My flat was on his way home. When I said goodbye, I opened up my door and the last thing I remember was consciously being able to throw myself across my bed, but lost consciousness enough to hear what was going on around me. Visualize.

There I am lying on my stomach, fully dressed in formal attire. My head was turned sideways with eyes forced shut. My right ear was facing the ceiling and my left ear was buried in the pillow. My arms were aligned at either side of the body as my legs were off the ground stretched out horizontally. In that state of consciousness, I was paralyzed, but could hear everything around me. And in the distance, I could hear voices approaching me louder and louder. I then felt a whirlwind as I finally could make out a voice which seemed very authoritative and powerful. It said to what I perceived was a force with an evil agenda, *"you will not harm him."*

I could feel the wind stir nothing short of a cyclone. I felt like I was in the vortex of a tornado – like a pressure field of some sort. I could hear myself screaming loudly though I could not get up despite how hard I tried. I merely surrendered. I heard another force screaming but I could not understand what was stated. I fell gradually into a deeper darkness and could hear nothing. I then felt out-of-body seeing myself on the bed, just lying their face-down. The voice then told me, *"you died tonight, but you will arise in the morning."* I felt myself open my eyes and could see everything in my dorm room but was overly-fatigued to get up so I fell asleep.

When I woke up the following morning, I was amazed at what I saw. As stated earlier on, I experienced feeling caught up in some centrifugal force – an atmosphere that was pressure packed. Now the evidence surrounded me. The light blue, gummy material that was used to glue decorative posters around my room became useless. They all were on the floor. A few books even fell over from the shelf in front of my desk where I completed assignments. I could believe that just perhaps one or two would detach because of some unusual gusts of wind, but when I looked over to the one window, I had in my dorm room, it was closed-shut from a cool English night. I knew had I opened it I will have caused the heating for my room to shut off.

Something extraordinary happened and that is perhaps why I was blinded by whatever presence was there.

Maybe I will have died that evening if allowed to wake up. Looking back, too, it is beginning to make a lot more sense as to what most likely happened.

Weeks before one of two Hindu sisters enlightened me as to the caste system of Hinduism. Before I arrived in England, I knew about Hindus, but I knew nothing much about their religion, in particular, nor did it really interest me. It must be borne in mind that I grew up under the principles of Christianity, so I thoroughly was convinced that God alone is my Creator.

Yet, I had a mother who understood the value of being open to other points of view including different religions since she attended school in England from very young. I was just too lazy to explore. And if I discovered information that needed some clarity, I could always go to mommy who discussed it to make me think and make it make sense.

I could remember the discouraged state of mind that caused me to be given the invitation that would further open my eyes to a spiritual difference. My friend somehow sensed that I was going through a lot. I was. I think it might have been along the lines of missing home. Being in law school was often challenging. It required discipline and I was not good at that. However, I managed to be punctual with deadlines although created a free spirit to be dreamy.

Curiosity made me do it. I loved learning new things from a very early age. When my friend told me she had a gift, my eyebrows raised. I wanted to know about this gift that she was willing to share and use. She convinced me that

I was feeling a bit down, that she could tell me why, and provide some advice and comfort. She invited me to her apartment, and it was nothing out of the blue. I had been there several times before. Please take your mind out of the gutter.

One time I remember going over and complaining that I was a bit under the weather. That is when I learned about the healing qualities of turmeric, honey and lemon mixed in water. It actually works. It worked deliciously.

It was a regular day and I knocked on the door of the flat to be let in. Inside my friend's bedroom, a table was set. On the table there was a cloth that contained something tied with a rope. My friend told me earlier that she is Brahmin – the highest of the Hindu caste consisting of nobles and priests. She shared that she possessed a gift of the third eye. When I saw this finely wrapped-whatever in fine cloth and roping I thought to myself this must simply be a part of it.

There was also a glass bowl of water and a selection of gorgeous stones and gems beside a stack of over-sized cards. The room was inviting and smelled of rich spice. I remember my friend holding the bowl with two hands – palms open and cupping around its circular shape. Her head was bowed as if to prepare for a meditation. She then untied the roping around the cloth and shortly after some very beautiful stones emerged. They were made to tumble into the bowl by hands and the process of holding the bowl was repeated.

My friend, then, asked me to put my hands in the bowl and breathe deeply to relax. After a short period, she told me to take my hands out and would put her hands in after touching the bowl and briefly initiated a more passionate meditation.

As soon as she put her hands in the bowl, like a person possessed her eyes grew very wide and they began darting left, right, upward, downward and they danced as if she was seeing things all too fast.

She closed her eyes and took her hands out of the water and asked me to open both my hands keeping them face up. Her hands pressed against mine. I felt nothing, but I could tell her sight was seeing a different dimension because as soon as she was done, she was able to tell me truths from I was a child up to that day. I never told her any of those things, but the tapestry revealed spoke to her gifting and led me to believe that she was divinely favored.

She then consulted her cards with very strange depictions that matched what she stated by her linking the imagery to what was happening. The cards were also used to tell me what I would experience in the future. It cannot be said with all honesty that I can remember everything that was said pertaining to my future, but what can be confessed is that everything related to my past was brought to the table. Before I left that day, it was stated that she will send a comforter to my bedside, and it will visit at the appropriate time. I actually appreciated what she said and left thrilled about the experience.

Now if we are to look at what happened from a Christian perspective, my friend was a witch or reader of tarot since her method of communication exemplified the occult. It would be further stated that I opened my spirit to a demonic attack, as our bodies are temples for spirits to express their existence. Because of this, it would be claimed that I allowed myself to be a portal for possibly evil spirits to enter.

The occurrence on the night of my moot event was not long after. So the possible truth is either the comforter sent was an evil force wanting to harm me or the force that fought to protect me. I would say that nothing has been fully proven. Either protection was sent or fear was inflicted.

Also, it is undisputed that my friend's gifting – her third eye as she put it – is equal to that of the Christian Prophet or Seer. The only difference is we do not consult cards since on the surface, it is considered tarot. While it is arguable that all friends do not always have one's best interest at heart, it is more likely than not that my Hindu friend had good intentions than none at all.

The most fascinating of revelations to my mind in terms of who the Creator is manifested in a vivid vision I had at the age of twenty-three. It is certain that many of you would think I went crazy or that I had a simple dream which required that I relax already. I needed not be validated then and certainly I am not in need of validation now. I know I am sane. But my life had not been the same since the vision I now share.

For many years I kept spiritual experiences to myself from fear that I will be called crazy. Yet, I am mindful that Noah of old was considered crazy when he had the vision of the awful flood. The people of the time thought he was a nut-case, and I even might have thought the same way had I lived back then. The huge Ark being built will have been the icing on the cake. What was Noah doing when he built that big, big boat? Yet, his story inspires me to be brave, as I convey my truth. Indeed, it is seemingly far-fetched, but I have no reason to tell a lie when I know that a Creator that smites a liar is quite real. And so I am guided.

It was a day I hung out with a close friend. As she reads my words just as you are, she will know who she is. Of course, I mean Nouria. I am beaming because she is my first ever godson's mother from Kinshasa, Democratic Republic of Congo. There was a spot we frequented at University to have a cup of coffee and donuts with icing and rainbow sprinkles. I blame her for the craving. She had an interesting palette because she introduced me to prawns, table water crackers and sharp cheese. I enjoyed her cooking especially because her native Congolese dishes comprised of a larger selection of meat. We are inseparable to date.

When we finished meeting up after having a blast of a time as usual, the blue-eyed server who tended to my order before Nouria and I met up would be used to demonstrate a very spiritual reality. In fact, the brown-eyed helper, too, was used as well as the green-eyed patron. All eyes collectively – all of them would come to tell an unforgettable story. I went home.

I remember everything like it was yesterday. I see myself – a young, vibrant 23-year-old student – somewhat tired as the evening approached. I can see him dropping his backpack, taking a deep breath, and fixing his body upright on the bed against the cold wall. As he sits there, his eyes are piercing and transfixed on his fat, lazy law books sitting recklessly on bookshelves and mimicking the characteristics of humans stuck in sloth – bent into shapes of surrender. It was a calm environment. There was no temptation to study. The atmosphere was peaceful and conducive to rest.

As I sat on the bed in a deepening trance, I decided to grab my MP3 player putting air buds in ears to help me lull myself to sleep. I chose the electronic album, *"Nonstop"* by Julio Iglesias and selected the song, *"Ae Ao."* From a child I loved that song. I lie down on my back and felt myself drift to sleep.

But before going to that black place where you go for sound rest, I could hear the music playing far above, but the sounds hovered over me like a cloud. I felt my spirit drifting in what appeared to be its own tomb. I was detached but alive. Could it be my soul?

Then I heard a voice that sounded like a gently flowing river with a touch of thunder calling my name. His voice incorporated every sound of nature known. The voice said, *"Sleep."* I then heard, *"Hold onto my voice, and sleep."* I had never heard the voice so distinctly before, but I was not afraid. I knew that I needed not to be afraid although I was not told that I should not be afraid. The voice sounded familiar and I could trust the voice, but I was not told to trust it either. It just felt natural to do so. It felt like this voice was so powerful yet calming enough to trust and not to question it. The voice said, *"Sleep."*

Renowned Singer, Julio Iglesias, the father of Enrique Iglesias, has a very euro-romantic appeal being gifted with a beautiful voice. The chorus of the song starts with the expression, *"Ae, Ao,"* which invites a roar of African-ess. When I heard the lyrics, *"Ae Ao,"* I could see symbols across my vision appear like hieroglyphics in different colors until I could see it written in full vision upon textiles of rock. To that end, the volume of my MP3 player was at its highest. Then the volume was lowered becoming faint to hear the voice tell me, *"I am Alpha and Omega"* – I then could see the actual symbols across my mind's space although my eyes were closed. Then when I saw the Omega symbol, He said, *"I am Infinity."*

Gradually, the omega symbol turned to the infinity sign. And the circular movement showed almost a computer-vivid imaging of DNA. I then witnessed a fast flash of symbols of what would appear to be ancient alphabets to a more recognizable set of Roman letters and numerals.

What was fascinating is although I saw a flash, I felt like I wrote these symbols before, as if I were taught it back in time. He then said, *"I am Jehovah, your Creator – Yahweh. I am the Beginning and the End. I was here from the beginning of time. I am that I am – the Creator of every creature made, and I am everything."*

At that time, the music, and words *Ae Ao* had become retarded and slowed down to almost one mystical sound. I was in darkness and surrounded by the most divine rendition of sounds I have ever experienced alive. I heard the voice say, *"This is the very beginning."*

Then emerging in a type of daydream with my eyes wide shut, I saw the scene replay when the server got my coffee hours earlier that day, and as I paid for it looking directly into his deep blue eyes. It was at that point that the voice told me, *"I was within the eye of that blue-eyed person, and I created the seas."* I felt myself pulled through the pupils of that person and I could hear the deep blue. He then explained, *"I created every fish of the ocean, lakes, rivers, and seas. This is the very beginning."*

I saw a school of fish approach me and when I focused on one, I saw, in a flash, every fish made as the voice repeated that He was the Creator of every fish made. I felt pulled upward from the depths of the sea and when I was taken out of the water, I could see the birds in the air. I heard the voice describe, *"I am the Creator of the heavens, the blue skies, the clouds, the planets and the universe. I am the Sun, the Moon, and the Stars. I am every bird."*

At that time, I saw what would appear to be flashes of birds that the voice confirmed, *"Was every bird He made."*

I started to feel sucked back to Earth. Then it felt like I stepped backwards from out of a dark person with brown eyes. The voice continued, *"I am in the brown-eyed person. I created the Earth, from the dirt of the ground. I am every brown-eyed person."*

The voice continued, *"I created the Heaven and the Earth, and I am the eyes of the green-eyed person – from the brown of the roots and barks of wood from the trees, I am the grass, to the leaves held by those branches on the trees. I created the animals upon the land! I created everything."*

As the voice declared it, I felt like I was introduced to every flora and fauna on the face of the Earth. It is difficult to explain, but it was as if I was taken back to the time and though the voice spoke in mere seconds, I lived every single moment.

The vision took me back to the darkness and I could hear mystical sound again. I felt as if I were drifting afloat. And then the voice said, *"I created the first tribe; I am the Sun and their god."*

At that moment I was taken to a civilization and out yonder, I could see many people on an open field of grass dancing harmoniously. I felt like I possessed one of the people in worship and I became that person. The people around me appeared to be both Indian-black in appearance and we worshipped passionately in a type of synchronized, passionate dance.

There were hundreds of us dressed in natural, dried grass and straw material. We were all on our knees and I felt myself bow on my forehead stretching forward to grab a full amount of soil in either hand. We then pulled ourselves up vertically with hands at either side, turning our heads left then right. We then threw the soil mixed with grass and plant roots in the air. Everything came back down to fall on our upper torsos because we would curve our backs extending our hands to a near horizontal direction behind us. Then we would pull ourselves back up with all our strength and assume the bowing position over and over screaming *"Hoo-Ha."* It sounded like a Southern chain gang on the beat in a furious rhythm. I could see their lives as I felt I relived every moment of a past life. I felt I lived among them. The voice confirmed, *"Everyone was formed from the first garden."*

He then repeated that He existed from the foundation of time. Then I saw a flash of changing faces that seemed to represent every race starting from pitch black skin to the palest of white skin. Next, he expressed, *"I am in the eyes of every person."*

Thereafter, I was taken back to the darkness – the peace and sounds that reopened my vision of what would appear to be Egypt. I saw the pyramids and what would also appear to be thousands of men and women – but the presence of men was more evident. I saw their clothing that revealed bareness matched with large and bold jewelry. As the voice narrated His creation through the passage of time, I felt reintroduced to various civilizations and relived past lives understanding them in detail.

I relived the brutality during the times of slavery, the Holocaust and the world wars, piracy, and deadly tribal conflicts throughout the passage of time. And as the smoke of it all cleared, I ascended out of it and was brought to the Agrarian Age; then the Victorian era, the 1920s to the current. As the vision closed. I was taken to different lands across the world and wore the garb of every religion and ascended to see the planet in what felt like outer space. The voice then, concluded, *"I am the Universe; let all my creation worship me."*

I knew it was over. It felt like a movie and I wanted to cry because I did not want the experience to end. I did not want that wonderful feeling to leave and disappear for good. I did not want to come back to life itself. It had nothing to do with unhappiness – it had everything to do with discovered gladness that goes against human comprehension.

I pleaded with the voice to let me stay and was told that we will meet again soon. Each time a statement was made the voice would say, *"Awaken"* and I ascended one level higher into consciousness, to a grayer void asleep. I felt exhausted and dehydrated but got up in shock thinking loudly in my mind, *"What the hell just happened?"* It must have been a glimpse of the God of Many Faces.

CHAPTER FIVE
His Omnipotence

When we attempt to describe the Almighty Creator – to use the word omnipotent means that He is super-powerful! To be crowned a King or an Emperor as a human being is considered the most powerful position on Earth. To think that God – the Universal Creator, breathes life into those who hold these positions should make us bow or curtsy in reverence! Is it not required to do so before an earthly King or Queen? What makes it any different for the Heavenly King?

Indeed, as brothers and sisters, worldwide, we call Him names which reverence His omnipotence based on what our parents and family tell us to believe and/or the influence of the various religions or non-religious belief taught in our locations of birth.

Another time I was having a very interesting conversation with a work colleague of mine. We discussed what we believed in and she shared that she calls the Heavenly Father *"Yahweh"* – the Jewish name meaning God but was raised Christian.

I started calling God, Yahweh, as well as Jehovah and Jah. What was especially mind blowing was she felt that the use of *"God"* is Supreme but felt that there were many gods or aspects of the Source. Capitalizing the *"G"*, she further clarified, only symbolizes that God is the *"God of gods."* We both grew up in The Bahamas, so her take was so intriguing. To sum it up we concluded that it is better to think of ourselves as spiritual-Christian as opposed to restricting our faith to one religion. We agreed that His omnipotence cannot be boxed in. It made a lot of sense and was a discussion that had enhanced my spiritual development.

God, or whomever you might call Him is the Father of all – the Source. He is the overall Ruler of the Heaven and Earth realms – everything in it and beyond the cosmos – seen and unseen, discovered, and undiscovered through infinity and beyond. One of my favorite writings is called, *"Desiderata"* written by Max Ehrmann in 1927. It was expressed:

> "You are a child of the universe,
> No less than the trees and the stars.
> You have a right to be here.
> And whether or not it is clear to you,
> No doubt the universe is unfolding as it should.
> Therefore, be at peace with God,
> Whatever, you conceive Him to be."

Additionally, William Ernest Henley asserted in his poem, "Invictus:"

> "Out of the night that covers me,
> Black as the pit from pole to pole,
> I thank whatever gods may be,
> For my unconquerable soul"

Having analyzed the moving words of both Poets, it is clear they acknowledge a Higher Source. Ehrmann identifies God, but added the pivotal words, *"whatever you conceive him to be.*" This shows that Ehrmann believes in God but acknowledges that we, the children of the Universe, do also call Him by other names.

In contrast, Henley does not plainly state his belief in God, but makes a general claim thanking, *"whatever gods may be"* for his unconquerable soul. His words highlight somewhat of a collective understanding that there is a higher source responsible for creation. But I will further use Henley's poetic words to further demonstrate how we can find the realization that God is Almighty.

Relax. Take three deep breaths. A good way to find God is by reentering the first void – pitch black. It would be worth it to close your eyes and simply meditate, erasing any form of anything that enters vision or any education that enters the brain.

Just go back to that black place. That place called your mother's womb. That place where the only music were the sounds of your mother talking, protecting and feeding you, the humming of her voice and the love you could feel even if you never met her.

The sounds of the outside world must have been faint, near mystical, because the wall of the inner and outer wombs serves as a barrier against anything that did not sound inviting. Besides, we all played in amniotic fluid, so do recall going for a swim in warm water. Hold on to that altered sound. Our parents could be having the wildest argument, but we heard music and the music of all who greeted our mothers.

Every bit of understanding was birthed in that peaceful environment. Before meeting our parents and being formally introduced to the world, who knew us? We know we enter the world through our mothers as we are implanted by our fathers. It must mean that the male was created first and this male needed a female in which to nest his seed. Who created that first man? And who created that first woman? Every human being who has graced this Earth came from one man and one woman.

No human being is capable of creating that original seed just as it is impossible for mankind to produce the divine coding of every flora and fauna known. So who created the zygote to become the embryo to become the fetus? The newborn with a selected gender becomes the toddler to become the child and teenager to become the adult to become old and die? Who guides evolution? Your deepest thought would draw you to light – the Universal Light of the Creator just as powerful as the Sun – the source of Life. Yet, He created the Sun, too.

Science describes that the foundation of everything are cells. These cells are primarily composed of protons, electrons and neutrons. They are electric by nature. Is it safe to conclude, then, that they are forms of light? If they are forms of light and the Universal Father is the Lord of Light, then is He not capable of creating it?

I am unsure that anyone can weaken the claim that the creation as we know it is an intelligent design that required a detailed process that began eons upon eons ago.

In fact, the Creation as we know it continues to evolve which is inspired by what is already created.

Moreover, our realities show us that our Creator has constructed an environment to survive, explore and admire. In its simplicity we are able to appreciate the good, bad and the ugly. We recognize that we are a part of a food chain and that everything works together as the planet spins. There is good and there is evil – there is conscience or the lack thereof which guides morality. There is life and there is death.

From the initial seconds when we are born, to minutes to the hour, time is quantified until the moment we die. Twenty-four hours is a day, twelve hours of daytime and twelve hours of nighttime. There are seven days in a week and fifty-four weeks is a year over the course of 12 months. Each month consists of 28 to 31 days. A year might seem long, but it is literally 525,600 minutes and 10 of them is a decade and there are 100 decades in a millennium.

It was a new millennium when I found it strange that my 12th grade homeroom teacher called me a millennial graduate because I officially left High School in 2000. I also remember the creepy feeling that would overwhelm me when I entertained the Y2K argument.

Apparently, it was the end of the world and there was going to be a crash of every computer known. I dreaded the thought of December 31st, 1999, 11:59pm. and anticipating the clock striking midnight. I do recall praying on my face that all will be well. I was about to die! But I would live pass

11:59 p.m. beyond which my mid-twenties explained life and death with a greater emphasis on the latter.

The mysterious recap revealed no church scene to review my Aunt Val's funeral, but instead I was shown the scenario in the graveyard. I could hear the saddening, *"Ashes to ashes, dust to dust"* ritual and saw myself as a child throw into the grave a white rose. And as I threw the white rose it felt like I became the white rose. The landing of the rose made me feel like I was placed in a casket and as I lie on my back, with its cover closed, I felt trapped. I felt the slab of concrete placed on my casket that would close my grave. I also could hear the dirt hitting the casket and slowly the noises of sorrow and finality grew faint. It was me and the voice of the Eternal Comforter. I heard, *"you are all the same."*

At that point I saw every person in attendance flash before my very eyes at both funerals. I then felt like I was burning and the stench of death slowly strangled me. I could feel my skin rip and crawl with maggots. It felt like a quilt over me. I could hear myself scream, but I was unable to go anywhere. I could hear people crying again and praying. I heard sorrow. All I could yell in this new state of being was, *"help me."* I endured that process for what seemed forever, but it eventually stopped. I heard, *"this is death. Your hell is your soul becoming free. Arise."*

I could feel myself detach floating through the top of the casket above my grave as if I was invisible and I was sucked into a light of absolutely, indescribable majesty and music. I now know why some people believe that the spirits of their ancestors are twinkling as the lives of stars across an open sky. For many of you it was another vivid dream. However, I have had many wondrous dreams, but more profound ones, I deem as visions. It definitely spoke to the "simplistically-complex" phenomenon of death.

Why exactly would I want to talk about that vision you might ask. The answer is to prove that via the Creator's omnipotence, He holds the key of life and death. The power is in His possession and knowing this can cancel those awful feelings surrounding death. This knowledge should provide a degree of comfort that surpasses human understanding. Why? We all must die after a fairly short time on Earth. Our mission here is not to impress others especially monsters who make us feel valueless! Rather, we are here to enjoy life for what it is worth – to bloom in the blessing of being alive.

How is it that people can glorify money believing that wealth is attained by a wicked capitalist agenda? The tragedy is that it collapses over and over again. Will we ever identify that the brain is responsible for the creation of Capitalism? Will we ever realize that the lust and greed for money is the biggest sin against ourselves? And further the brain completes the man in terms of Biology, but made by a source that should be given the gratitude!

In other words, it has nothing to do with humanity. We are not blessed by the businesses we work for to earn a salary. We are blessed by the Almighty who has blessed business-owners to pay themselves a paycheck, and fair wages to their employees who have very well earned it.

It should not be said that human beings, alone, are the direct providers of prosperity and happiness because the same humans can also be the reason why a lot of people remain impoverished and disenfranchised. We are mere vessels that house good and evil spirits. I should like to think that a Creator who has made us does not want to see us unfairly treated and suffering. He is not a God of Haves and Have Nots. What a strictly human view!

For example, think of all souls as a universal currency valuing 100. There is no other number. One hundred as a percentage means perfection. We cannot and shan't debate that we are all equal. In terms of any international currency, the maker of money knows that it will endure a number of trials and tests either to add value or devalue that currency of the time. Indeed, the competitive kingdoms run by Satan and its demons will attempt to devalue God's currency. Yet, our currency, Under Jehovah, cannot and will not change like a dollar remains a dollar and a yen remains a yen.

Now I know why mommy cries when she hears the song, *"My Redeemer Lives."* Such powerful lyrics so beautifully portray the Great "I Am" – the Ruler of the Universe, who bears the Light over darkness. If you sincerely believe in the Creator or like the Poet Max Ehrmann puts it, *"whatever you conceive Him to be"*, you walk in your truth.

If your Father in heaven be most powerful, then that means you are made in His image and likeness possessing power in your truth. We are royal and appointed to this status through the divine. If it is found that the Creator is difficult to believe in, it should be realized that He is spirit and unseen – too powerful to conceive. He is genderless.

He is called He because of the patriarchal concept that the male on Earth – being created first is the strongest symbolism of the family structure. Because the Creator is not human, but far superior, this cannot be sexist as He can be expressed as both male and female in one. He is nurturing. Because He is a caring King of kings, we deserve to evolve into our truth of divine royalty and power.

Famous Singer *Shaggy* in his song, *"Strength of a Woman"*, questions it humorously. His voice captures the wonder of whether God is actually a woman. The metaphor he maintains throughout the song speaks to the baffling nature of God because even King Solomon declared that the ways of a woman are far from finding out.

The power to which is being referred is not the superficial power that often invites pomp and pageantry. It is an authority of self-assurance through which our place in life does not have to be known by force. This power is known by mere presence because true power is asserted in peace. It is walking in that spiritual dignity that does not require the acceptance of mankind and society. The only validation required is by a being that people know or might not know. In this knowledge, our mere actions and speech will cause a special fragrance to spread throughout any given space.

People with evil plans, thus, will recognize that good works will pay off. There will be the internal battle that there is something about that man or there is something about that woman. The truth is the Source of this grace is intangible so only an intangible attack can offend or destroy it. In the sphere of the Spirit, you are only open to destruction if you are not linked to the Source.

I can vividly recall an incident when the omnipotence of the Almighty was demonstrated on a visit to Toronto which I will share shortly. I am sure that many more examples presented themselves during my lifetime thus far. This one, though, seems so appropriate to share at this point. I can remember visiting many churches during my childhood. The visits that stood out were the many prayer meetings and Bible studies I had the honor of attending. I might not have understood everything that was being taught at that time, but I did begin to realize the power of prayer. Some people were very passionate when they prayed, and I could feel emotions that cannot be properly justified by human words. I was able to experience energy on frequencies that are beyond this world. I know that I know that the Creator of creators is real.

Before Aunt Val died, I travelled often to The Bahamian capital of Nassau because Aunt Val lived there with her husband and two daughters. I resided in Freeport, Bahamas. Most of the world, in my experience, seems to think that The Bahamas is only Nassau and Paradise Island. But the country, in fact, is an archipelago of 700 islands. I am from the north on an island shaped like a ship, known for its golf courses, mangrove-packed creeks and underwater caverns. The Bahamas is magical and there is no place I'd rather live unless there was an imminent threat that the islands, collectively, would sink like Atlantis!

Speaking of Atlantis, the high-end resort known also as Atlantis located on Paradise Island, Bahamas, was my playground as a child. I played there long before the resort was built in Dubai. Bahamians are a blessed people even though sometimes we forget it.

To leave this paradise for greener pastures is not necessarily a bad thing. There are some of us that move and do very well because it was purposed to be that way. And then there are those of us who are absolutely infatuated with the country. We can be heard complaining profusely that changes need to happen or that the government needs a clearer vision. But so do the citizens of countries across the globe. The pasture is never really greener on the other side – it is merely different!

As a young child I had left turquoise-blue pastures many times to experience deeper blue pastures that could be seen as lakes, rivers and waterfalls that I never had before seen. Another one of my aunts to whom I grew closer is Aunt Cherry. Yes, the fruit, but none of my family would ever be heard calling her Gwendolyn or Gwen. Who is that?

Back then she lived in Brampton, Ontario with her husband, Gavin now deceased. Aunt Cherry was very nurturing from young because she was made responsible, with the full support of my maternal grandfather, to raise several, younger siblings. My maternal grandmother died young. My grandfather will have met another woman having more children, but took care to ensure that his children beforehand were raised without want or need for anything.

His children born in marriage remained in the matrimonial home while he lived with his new significant other and extended family. He was an excellent father, I understand, and I am certainly proud to know that such a giant of a man was my grandfather. He died when I was about four years old. Louis Isaacs Sr. made me a firm believer that men should take care of their responsibility no matter how challenging their circumstances become.

Aunt Cherry to this day is a very refined woman and hostess. She makes a mean sandwich and I can assure you, if you visit her, you will be well fed and feel welcome. Her home was always tastefully decorated. In my younger years she lived in a very large, cozy home with a huge backyard extended by what appeared to be an open field beyond the low, logged fence. The front of the house was quaint because it resembled a snap from an upscale homes catalogue. Later she would move from that location to a lovely, townhouse-like accommodation. I stayed their once or twice, but have not visited Canada in years.

A memory that stands out at the big house still causes Aunt Cherry to think that I am fond of telling tall tales. I was about twelve at the time. One day she went to the grocery store, and before she left, she told me to ensure I make myself something quick to snack on because she would be back to prepare a meal. I was a plump kid and she made time to ensure I ate on time. The meals were always on point - scrumptious. One of my favorite dishes she would make is penne pasta and a homemade sauce in which she would incorporate Italian sausage – yummy!

So she went out and I decided to boil water in a pot so that I could cook two hot dogs – two or possibly three would fill me. Don't judge me; I loved to eat! So I put on the stove and also the water to bring it to a boil. Tyler, the family boxer-dog entered and I began to play with him. Tyler was such a human.

At Aunt Cherry's, it was rare that we would enter the house through the front door. We would usually drive to the back entrance into what was called the *"Mud Room."* It was appropriate because walking indoors from the snow was oftentimes a *"muddy experience."* So we left our wet boots or muddy shoes in that room and proceeded into the living room just before the kitchen. Also, it was a place to store odd knick-knacks.

On this occasion, I had to go into the Mud Room to get something to, *"out my munchies."* So I remember opening the thick oak door and the cold hit me like blocks. It was summer as I can recall, but it was chilly outside for some reason. What I did not know is that Tyler followed me into the Mud Room and shut the door which was locked. I did not think that the door was locked right away until I got what I needed and tried to reenter the house.

When I turned the door knob I became petrified – petrified enough not to be angry and literally poison Tyler, but petrified enough to want mommy and release hot piss!

All I could think was that the house was going to burn down and it was going to be my fault. The sheer horror that I was feeling was certain to win an Academy Award. The scene that was unfolding was dramatic. There I am with a Boxer – and if you know how Boxers look, they are not the most attractive-looking dog. They could frighten you if they appear unexpectedly. I could smell Tyler's fart because he was nervous too. He could sense my fear. The tears began to fall, but Tyler could only look at me as if he was retarded – his tongue seemed extra-long at that moment flapping over the right side of his mouth. I did not know if I wanted to scream or cry.

I knew that I had to pray to God. I knew that the water would boil out and cause problems. I felt an urge to pray. I closed my eyes and began to call on the angels. I started to speak in tongues the prayer was so severe. I got up, grabbed a stick and headed for the door. You could not tell me I was not Moses on the journey to part the Red Sea. I remember saying, *"Father God, in the name of Jesus Christ of Nazareth"*, and at that point, I took the stick that looked like a walking cane of some sort, jammed the end into the groove to the bottom of the door and shouted, *"Open!"* as I pushed the stick downward holding it with two hands. When I did that, the solid oak door lifted and nearly broke open off its hinges. To this day I know that it could not be of my own wisdom. Even Tyler looked and doggie-replied in confusion – I had to calm down Scooby-Doo.

I know looking back at it that God's power was used. It baffles me to know how it happened, but it did. When I went into the kitchen the pot was empty and it began to burn the pot. Even when I showed Aunt Cherry the evidence of her house possibly being burned down, and what happened to prevent it, she did not believe me. My recollection of events will not have changed, and I am certain that I was not dreaming. Aunt Cherry if she can recall will confirm that the day in question did in fact occur.

But Aunt Cherry could not believe that her solid oak door could be opened by a twelve-year old in the way in which it happened. It was too incredible – too Bible story and full of creative imagination, I suppose. If God could grace the Earth, I would say it happened all over again. If Tyler's bark could translate to English, he would confirm it happened too.

God demonstrated His omnipotence by granting His child wisdom after prayer. This, in turn, defied what was more easily acceptable, that is, to let the house burn down. Instead, God's omnipotence opened the impossible oak door!

It reminds me of another occasion when the Creator emerged like magic to show His existence and might, but that He can be playful too. Daddy's sister, Aunt Vandolyn, and three of her children came to Freeport on a visit. She brought her two sons and daughter along. Her daughter and I were close in age and even closer cousins.

One day we went outside in the backyard to swim in the pool. At that time, we had a patio, and you would walk up steps to go into the pool. It had a unique design. Before a terrible hurricane one year we had many trees that bore fruit in the backyard like scarlet plums, Persian limes, avocado, and mangoes. The trees were always pregnant of mangoes – peach, mangola and hairy mangoes. They were delicious and sometimes branches would hang over the deep end of the pool like a tree was handing mangoes to those fortunate enough to swim in the deep end.

As children that was paradise on Earth, so my cousin and I began swimming and playing. There were a few dark clouds forming and we sensed that the weather would worsen and start raining. We started to feel the warning drops of drizzle on our heads poking us that is will rain. My cousin managed to come out of the pool first as I swam after her in hot pursuit. It was a friendly game of tag. As I approached the steps to come out of the pool, I could see my cousin looking up at the sky as if she had seen a ghost. That is perhaps what got me out of the pool quickly since I was curious to see what caught her attention.

As soon as I took my right foot out of the water and turned around, I saw a waterspout coming down from the clouds and land in the pool. Waterspouts are not uncommon in The Bahamas, as they usually can be seen out on the open ocean far into the horizon. But this water tornado formed and landed in the pool and started to stir the water in a clockwise direction as it danced on the surface. It looked like a scientific display of an ocean storm at Epcot. The cyclone lifted up and took itself back into the sky. Looking back at it we should have taken cover, but we were understandably too overwhelmed to move. We ran into the house, thereafter, screaming for any adult absolutely stunned by what we witnessed.

The Creator's power can be experienced in the storms we experience during our lifetimes. When we hear the wind blow, we know that is His breath can be even more powerful. When the thunder roars, we could hear His voice knowing that He is designed to command and when there is lightning it is the evidence that He is the Great Ruler of Light. Natural disasters are reminders that He is the Master of our Fate, The Wondrous and Omnipotent!

CHAPTER SIX
And Omniscience

If Albert Einstein was impressive to the extent of shaking the world, it is no great wonder why God is far from understood. He remains almighty and omniscient. What this means is that God is all seeing and all knowing. This is important when it comes to holding onto faith despite what we might be going through. Jehovah knows and has the power to brighten any situation. This should provide comfort to mankind.

Because God knows everything and there is no real limit to His knowledge, then it is safe to conclude that there is such a thing called destiny.

Around the age of thirty-six, I had composed a poem called, *"A Page from the Grateful"* in which it was written:

> Step graciously into the daybreak,
> Every moment is our last,
> Be at peace with humanity,
> And let bygones be the past;
>
> Setting eyes on the horizon,
> As minutes pass too soon,
> Through hours of endurance,
> To the summons of the moon;
>
> No matter how charged the path,
> Of earthquakes, hail, or rain,
> We will always emerge triumphant,
> Through the tsunami and hurricane;

Onto the deserts of disappointments,
And the quicksand of depression,
An oasis indeed draws near,
Under our Creator's protection;

We call Him **Many Names**,
Like Chukwu, Allah or God,
We're one people of many nations,
May equality be our sword!

Beyond the night's rest,
Another journey has begun,
Always strive to be thankful,
For the rising of the sun;

Since many lost that freedom,
As they die for it crave,
Stalked by the Grim Reaper,
Calling their spirits to the grave;

So, despite all we go though,
As there'll be many trials and tests,
To exist six feet above ground,
Is to know that we are blessed.

At the time that I composed that poem, I was inspired by the many challenges I had gone through in my life and despite them all, I overcame through God's grace. To my mind's eye, I went back to a particular low point when I had overcome a near death encounter with no real plan for the next move. The thing is no one truly knows when sickness will strike and nothing teaches you that lesson better than experience.

One tired evening I remember feeling very ill and extremely hot on the inside of my body. I was not feeling well, at all, and deep within I knew that something was quite wrong. I thought maybe if I went to sleep, I would feel better. Indeed, I fell asleep but when I woke up, I felt a hell-of-a-lot worse. Mommy came to my room to check up on me because she noticed that I was acting unusually strange.

I was drained and did not care to talk to anyone – not even mommy to whom I am so close! Those who know me well enough can attest that when I am in good spirits, I can be talkative and bubbly to a fault.

Although, I was trying my hardest to convince mommy that I would be alright, she refused to accept my appeal. She sensed something was wrong and was unprepared to leave me in that state. I got dressed with very little strength and felt like I would faint, but thankfully I did not. Mommy drove me to the hospital and spoke the whole time telling me that I should try my best to stay awake. I drifted in and out of a conscious "La La Land."

We had arrived at the hospital about fifteen to twenty minutes later and mommy started a melodrama because she knew that whatever I was going through needed immediate attention. Only mommy had a son that evening. Somehow, other sick sons and daughters did not matter anymore because I had arrived. It must have been that bad because somehow mommy's panic moved a nurse to wheel me in pronto to see a doctor. I was oriented enough to explain my symptoms. For some reason, the doctor was puzzled because he was unable to determine the cause of my extreme fatigue.

He had ordered a blood test and it was found that my blood was becoming dangerously septic. The nurse was ordered to put me on an antibiotic drip so as to treat my blood. She responded right away. I could remember the delicate connection of the IV into my bloodstream. To think that a small, plastic sac suspended by a long slender pole was fighting to keep me alive was troubling. Fortunately, I am not terrified of needles. I sat there like a pro and awaited the treatment allowing the nurse to do what was necessary without a flinch.

Shortly after being connected to my new lifeline, I could taste the antibiotics and it seemed to awaken me from the pull of a deep coma. It is like I got a burst of energy and became hyper in minutes. I had been sleeping for a while, but I could not feel better as my blood was getting more and more infected. When I reacted this way, the doctor said something dangerous is going on and he had to pinpoint exactly the root of the infection – and that is exactly what it was. It was not until the doctor asked me if I was feeling any pain did I notice that I felt a slight pain when I sat down. He made me take off my clothing to lie on my stomach and Great God Almighty when he pressed on the affected area, which was my hip, it really hurt!

Thankfully, due to thorough examination and consultation between a Filipino and African doctor it was discovered that I had a fistula in my lower rectum. This is a common possibility in that persons can get them when they strain on the toilet and injure the rectum by a tear or cut. Apparently, I remembered *"doing the two"* and cutting myself. I could recall the blood. Excuse my being too personal and gross, but I believe my truth is relevant here.

The aim really is to show you how merciful God is. Had it been written in my destiny that I should die that night – I will have undoubtedly been a goner! And by a cause that is not uncommon. Why those doctors in particular? What if they had not been so thorough? What if mommy thought that it was a normal fever? What if she was not so interested in how I was feeling and left me be?

In fact, it was the doctor's claim that had I not come when I did, a few hours later, I will have died because the infection was moving so rapidly. Indeed, from Septicemia! I was scheduled to undergo an emergency surgery the following morning to remove the fistula that burst and began poisoning my blood.

I can recall that night as tears flowed from my eyes thinking that I could have expired at home if mommy did not bring me to the hospital. That is destiny. I always say that mommy was blessed with a keen sense of discernment. She took heed to the red flags and moved swiftly and through God I am still alive.

The following morning, I went under the knife slowly nodding off from the anesthesia. I hated not being able to control falling sleep, but I knew that God had given doctors the wisdom to perform miracles. About an hour and a half later, I gradually arose from a deep sleep with a team of doctors encouraging me. I could hear voices in the distance saying, *"come on Angelo, wake up, come on you can do it. If you can hear us, wake up."* I slowly awakened and was advised that I could go back to sleep when I was ready.

I remained in hospital for 3 to 5 days to recover because the cut had to be dressed and kept clean. I was told how to clean the rather *"strange feel"* and because I did what I was told correctly and consistently, I healed with no infection and little to no scarring thereafter.

Now the question begs, *"How exactly does this experience tie in"?* It does – because we know thus far that not only is God omnipotent and most almighty, but He is also omniscient or all-knowing. He sees all things. The fact is I injured myself like so many others of Jehovah's children and became seriously infected. Yet God allowed me to live and allowed others to die, which is a testimony of His omnipotence – His infinite authority of life over death. My purpose on Earth had not been fulfilled and so with the Creator's unlimited authority, wisdom and mercy, He appointed the right doctors to assess the situation and repair it.

Only with His permission could I or anyone else carry out our assignments on Earth. We are a part of a great family in the never-ending story of life. That is why in the poem I end by saying, *"to exist six feet above ground is to know that we are blessed."* We should always strive to be grateful.

Progressively, having survived some years later, I now know exactly why I went through those series of events. It is said that hindsight is always 20/20. There came a day when I had regained my health and strength to seek a job. I would say that just perhaps at that juncture when I fell ill, it was convenient. I was not employed at the time having recently stopped working at an all-inclusive resort.

It was the end of 2009 – a very exciting year of opportunity under the then government of The Bahamas. The Minister of Tourism at that time had advertised a Tourism Apprenticeship inviting candidates from all over the country to apply. I did and received an answer that a general knowledge test must be passed in order to be interviewed. I was fortunate to have passed making the cut for a final interview through which I sailed reserving a spot to become a Tourism Apprentice.

The way it worked was that I was to be placed at three locations to learn how exactly Tourism works and was expected to write a report after two-month rotations. Tourism is a big deal in The Bahamas, as it is our leading industry accounting for 85% of the Bahamian workforce. So the apprenticeship lasted a total of six months.

It was an exciting experience to have worked at a boutique hotel, at the Ministry of Tourism itself and to have been employed by the local Tourism Board in Freeport, Grand Bahama. I had learned so much and discovered a talent in jingle writing. I wrote two jingles during my tenure, one of which was used for a seasonal training seminar and the other for an upcoming cultural festival. That same year, the festival was a huge success and it was a thrill to be a part of the project.

I scored highly in my certification exam and was deemed Valedictorian of the class and overall Top Apprentice for the island of Grand Bahama. Sadly, the government at that time lost the General Election in 2010 and, thus, my opportunity to be considered a permanent placement in the Ministry of Tourism was shattered. I tried many times to be employed by an industry that I grew to love, but the doors remained closed despite being qualified.

Looking back, while at the time I was most disappointed, it was the beginning of an illustrious career that has presented such an amazing and diverse experience. One door closed but others swung open. Pounding the pavement, I became a High School Teacher to teach English and Commerce at a school that is known for students with behavioral problems. That is where I learned that all students really want is a cool adult to teach and be flexible enough to listen and understand them. All that is necessary to accomplish that interchange is applying innovative methods in the classroom setting.

Moving from there, I graduated in a way to have had the unforgettable chance to teach the entire English faculty at a technical and vocational institute. It was there that I learned the different learning styles and how to make my classes more engaging and memorable. I had a blast.

When my contract ended there, I ventured into timeshare and vacation club sales. That is when I learned to sell myself rather than the product through the power of persuasion. It tested my faith because I relied on commission instead of a consistent paycheck. It would also lead me to a short period of operational management as well as legal and receptionist work within the vacation club industry.

The wealth of experience proved beneficial to my resume. I will forever be grateful. I would come to lose faith because days could go by without being paid and I did not like the discomfort that could linger from not receiving a steady paycheck. I reverted to what I knew best and that was teaching.

Then a hurricane destroyed the school that employed me, and I was forced to relocate to an island called Bimini, which is one of many beautiful islands in The Bahamas. There I worked as an Executive Concierge and learned hospitality at a fine level. It was a pleasure providing my services to guests from around the world.

Through that stint at the lovely hotel, I honed my hospitality skills. Also, my love for poetry was kindled just as the kindling of thoughts of the great Ernest Hemingway who frequented Bimini to write a number of bestsellers. Would you believe Dr. Martin Luther King wrote a number of his famous speeches there? Another hurricane would end my time at that hotel lounge that I graced daily with a smile. I was forced to find another job.

My biggest trial was again relocating to Freeport to decide exactly what I was going to do next. The lounge had been damaged and there was no way I could return until further notice. However, when the wait became too long to return to Bimini, I applied to a very prestigious resort in the capital and received word that I would need to fly in for an interview.

I got the job and was assigned once again as a Concierge. It was there that I learned the very extremes of conflict on the job and how to, albeit, maintain professionalism. I would not say that I always passed the test, but looking back, the journey had taught many ways to avoid it.

After leaving that resort, and being unemployed for a while, yet again, I found myself left with very limited choices because the economy was ailing. But thankfully a company hired me in customer service where I learned to deliver exceptional customer service outside the ambit of tourism and hospitality. It has been great up until this point and has created the foundation of considering entrepreneurship and other ways of branding myself to impact others in a more global way. This might not have happened if my career evolved within the Ministry of Tourism.

When we say God is omniscient – as His manufactured design, we are individually living out the reason we were born. He has given us gifts and talents and has molded a certain life for us. The Creator has given us a degree of free will so as to feel we are in control, but that control is inclined toward our nature that was carefully crafted by the Most-High. Every unique system of the human body is working as it should to express the animation of our spirit-beings. This unseen character is played out as we live daily.

Unfortunately, our spirit man cannot be appreciated with human eyes and, thus, a shell composed of skin spread over bones was created instead. We are to coexist as the story is being told. Our story in hindsight – forms history and the revelation of the rest will inevitably unfold. Time is constant and we are here reacting to a universal flow of time.

I remember a while ago I would state, *"Life is a drama of music and words."* As I age, I come to find out more and more that that is exactly what life is. Mommy would share that her grandma "Dotty," in turn, my great grandmother would say, *"Time ain't long as it has been"* just like Bahamians would agree that *"pig does grow hog"* (A pig, in time will become a hog." I agree, time "ain't" long at all.

On a more declaratory note, it has been explained that knowing our Heavenly Father's omnipotence – His almighty authority, should give us a sense of divine dignity; the added knowing of God's omniscience – His limitless knowledge, should provide comfort and wipe away all forms of fear and undue worry.

Once we can understand that God loves us and cares for us and our future, seeking His advice should be our mission. Worshipping and adoring the Creator should be our deepest desire because there is no other being that can remotely compare when it comes to His compassion, protection, and provision.

The Father in Heaven is the Genius of all geniuses, the Pastor of pastors the Guru of gurus, the Rabbi of rabbis – and the Professor of professors. Understand that the knowledge of God is infinite – a bottomless well of science and mysteries that infinitely remains untapped. Since this is the case we should do all that is necessary to consult Him. We must surrender to the state of a humble child who is passionate for knowledge. We can seek to be humble to find the inner peace as there is power in silence. This is where we can hear the Voice of the Almighty rather clearly.

Once we are convinced that He is the Source of endless might and knowledge our desire for his revelations will burn as hot as fire. Our sense of dignity and esteem will most certainly soar with the might of eagles, becoming well defined and evident as there will be no fear of the impossible.

Resting in the undisputed truth that God knows all things and being led by His spirit and advice promotes living a very happy and powerful reality. We begin to understand that everything is everything and what we endure, whether the experiences are good, bad, or ugly, we can accept that it is for the greatest good. Faith in God was demonstrated at one time in my life. I will never forget the turn of events for as long as I live.

I am sure that I was not more than eleven years old. The day that would change a childish perspective of fate was like any other day. I can recall having to go to school and carrying on with business as usual. There was nothing really extraordinary to talk about, as it was the same routine, but on a different day. Earlier that morning mummy convinced me that a guest was coming in from the United States to visit us for the weekend. Since this had happened several times before it was not incredible. All that was stated is that when I came home, I would be required to take a shower and then later in the evening, we would be going to the airport to greet the incoming guest.

When I arrived home, I could remember watching television because I had no homework. Everything seemed normal and to the back of my mind was the memory of what mommy said. So when I was told that I had to shower and get ready, I simply obeyed. I had a habit of taking a backpack with me everywhere I went because I loved music. At that time portable cassette players were in. You were not a kid if you did not have a portable cassette player. Gameboys and Game Gear came later.

Mommy and daddy were in the front seat of the family car as we drove to the airport. The weather was a bit dark and dreary and I could hear thunder every so often. I could also sense the weather was not the best for flying. There were no fears anyway because I was not travelling anywhere. I was more concerned about our guest who was flying in to visit us. From a child I was sensitive, and it is likely that I asked my parents if they thought the flight for our guest was smooth or not. Whatever their answer was I am sure I will have agreed because I was too young to know any better or to really care.

When we arrived at the entrance of the airport, mommy told me to go inside and look for the guest while she and daddy parked the car. I was gullible because I did not see it coming. I was sold on the idea that there was a guest coming through Arrivals at the airport. I knew where to look because I was accustomed to travelling a lot by then. There I am standing at Arrivals looking with all eyes. Had I been thinking I will have realized that I did not know for whom I was looking, but mommy assured me that the person would recognize me because the mystery guest knew me from birth and had seen recent photographs as I grew up. I was smart enough at least to ask questions, but I was naïve enough to fall for a lot.

What I had not realized is that at some point when I was not looking, my clothes were packed up and hidden from me because we were actually at the airport to board a flight. Mommy knew what I liked to wear so it was a breeze for her to pull off the scandal.

I noticed that no one else was coming out of the electrical sliding doors at Arrivals and no one recognized me so I thought that just perhaps the guest missed the flight. I set out logically, then, to find my parents and in perfect timing, I saw mommy and daddy headed in my direction. It still had not hit me that I was going away because the dumb words were uttered, *"You found the guest eh because no one came through the sliding door"* in a childish Bahamian accent.

Full-blonde, I looked at the bags thinking that the guest must have had identical luggage to ours because I never thought in my wildest imagination that I was going away to Miami until mommy and daddy blurted out, *"Surprise!"* I was beyond happy – it was instant euphoria. The visibly bad weather turned to sunlight and thoughts that anything bad could happen was erased from my mind.

There was a midnight flight between Freeport and Miami back then. It departed at exactly 12:00 a.m. I loved Miami and it only took a 35-minute flight to get there. Some of my best memories during my childhood were in Miami. I absolutely loved the Embassy Suites and their free breakfasts in the morning. The atmosphere was so playground and magical to me as a child. A quick meal at the food court in between shopping at the Westland Mall was a treat especially from *Manchu Wok*.

I could remember there being a very kind Asian lady who owned the outlet, and every time I visited the mall, I looked for her. She would always give me something free to eat. I remember those awesome dinners at Sizzler. I would eat steak like nobody's business and just live the good life that any child wanted.

We are seated on the aircraft finally. The passengers I am sure were eager to get to Miami just like me. I knew that it was another shopping trip that lasted for about 2 or 3 nights so I did not have too long to soak it all in.

Time went and we started blasting across the runway and finally lifted off the ground in a diagonal climb toward an open black sky. I was never a fan of that gravitational bullying – stay in your seat or else! There is always that powerless feeling until you are completely airborne and leveled out.

Moments into the flight were calming. I remember sitting in the window seat. Mommy was seated beside me in the middle seat and daddy sat in the aisle seat. Across the aisle was my father's bosom-friend who was a pilot and well-known businessman. He seemed pretty engaged with my parents until suddenly the ride started to get bumpy. The jolly conversation was no longer looking as jolly since adult faces grew concerned. The black and every-two-second flash of blue could no longer be seen outside the aircraft.

Like an omen across the stratosphere, there was a pale-pink glow in the clouds with a flash of blue lights. Then strings of water drew themselves horizontally on cabin windows like ghostly bear claws were ripping through. The flight was getting very bumpy and there were mini drops and quick jerks upward as if the plane really wanted to free fall. The thought of that happening was teasing passengers aboard like seeing hands about to tickle our bodies but the tickling never occurred. The turbulence got worse and worse. The panic and fear moved through the cabin like wildfire because the drops became more frequent so every drop might as well have been the last one to take us out of our misery.

At this point I was crying as I held onto mommy tight. If it got tighter I am sure she would gasp for air. I looked across to my father – and for once in my life I saw a blank stare that was similar to the stare his friend wore. They were deathly silent giving a very eerie expression that to my young mind could not be intended to help the situation – I was expecting a face of bravery, but instead I got Frankenstein. Daddy's friend seemed confident that the airplane should level out. When the aircraft ascended and descended here and there, he did question the need so even his expertise in flying was being challenged. He managed to be more realistic and concluded that everything should be alright and confirm the obvious that the weather must have been really bad. Um ... like did we not already know this?

What was more concrete was mommy soothing my fears by looking into my eyes and assuring that all will be just okay. For some strange reason, she seemed to be the calmest though, instinctively, I could tell she was scared as hell. Her maternal response was so settling. Her beautiful face convinced me that we would not plummet to our unfortunate deaths. She started to tell me little jokes from the past and managed to get me to smile and chuckle but still I could pee and fill gallon bottles by force! I had never felt so afraid in my life.

It was that drop immediately following that made the terror worse. That free fall for what seemed an eternity whispered that I would meet my Maker – I could see Jesus, as I screamed with a choir of primates. I closed my eyes since it seemed to be the best thing to do. Mommy grabbed onto me tighter as she began to pray aloud.

Mommy is a prayer warrior. She prayed as if commanding that the storm should leave us alone because all the passengers aboard were children of a Living God. I could hear the roaring of her voice as she prayed with every ounce of faith and every declaration like she was born of royalty from the very womb of the Universe.

We as human beings are entitled to be afraid and scream when we are scared of the unthinkable happening. All mommy did was pray. She prayed to God with strong conviction despite the danger that we were battling. If God be omniscient and we embrace that He knows everything – then if we are in a similar situation we ought to pray to that Ruler of our fate.

Nothing could happen to or for us, whether good or bad, without the approval of God. I could remember mommy appealing to His Throne and saying, *"not my will Lord, but your perfect will be done."* We know that God wants the best for us. We know that He does not want anything bad to happen to us, and if the flight that night had in fact crashed, then call it fate. It will have happened anyway. But shortly after the prayer went up, the blessing came down. The plane would also descend in Miami – and smoothly too.

I am human, and while I looked forward to a great trip ahead, I felt the temporary fear of returning back to Freeport on the same airline. What I took from it at that young age is the gratitude that God, in His infinite power and knowledge, continues to protect us regardless of our wrongdoings. He controls everything and found the mercy to extend life. That night I could have lost my life, but I did not.

Similarly, many souls have gone airborne and wound up dying from a fatal crash. The reality is planes fall out of the sky or crash tragically in some form of freak-accident. Persons never think they will die when they go onto an aircraft. Many even forget that it is the grace of God that takes them to and from destinations safely.

The little girl from Yemen who survived that crash, years ago, never knew that she would fall from the sky. When faced with her very life flashing in front of her, she never knew that she would have to tell her story that would amaze the world. These types of miracles are reminders of impossibilities made possible because nothing is impossible when we seek the Face of God.

CHAPTER SEVEN
God is Omnipotent, Omniscient and Most Omnipresent

I do not know why it is that I am hearing the song, *"Electric Slide"* by Jamaican Singer Marcia Griffith, but her lyrics inspire me to describe God as being, *like electric, He is near, over there and through the air.*

It is a song to which I got up and danced from I was a young child. Indeed, I am a fan of line dance and could be seen into the moonlight at the Count Basie Square in Port Lucaya, which was an outdoor entertainment spot on the island I grew up. I can remember those playful, breezy evenings on the weekend. The tourists and natives would dance together and have a great time.

The song will have been performed by the live band or by record and the moment it started, I was up and about. Interestingly, the thought of electricity is exactly what can be envisioned when we think of omnipresence.

God is powerful – He's electric – now Dougie-Dougie! Jehovah cannot be seen, held, controlled, or contained. God is the creator of power and light and is the source of life. God is not wanted; He is needed.

We are created to know that God is our Maker, and because it cannot be denied that a Higher Power exists even when we do not call it God, then clearly, He must know we are here. Thus, the Almighty Maker knows everything about us, just as a manufacturer knows its product. The inability to resist God's electric nature proves the truth that we need

Him since no one else knows the key when we cannot overcome.

The fact that *God is near, over there and through the air* is the very definition of omnipresent! God resides in eternity. In a poem I wrote called, *"Voice of Hope"*, I expressed the Christian perspective of the Almighty Creator. It was written:

> Out of the void
> I am neither male nor female,
> I am spirit,
> Dwelling in the hearts of men,
> Seemingly distant,
> But that I am not;
>
> I can roam in the bottomless pit,
> Of the disappointed,
> Brokenhearted,
> And ashamed;
>
> Throughout the battles of time,
> I have dried the eyes of people,
> And by hearing my voice,
> There has been victory;
>
> My highest appeals,
> Take me to the heavens,
> And before me,
> Is always my Father,
> Though oft unseen,
> He is God;

His gentle embrace,
Calms the deepest of fears,
He is even my sole comfort,
And despite the power I bring,

He is the true Light and Salvation;
A world away,
I tread among you,
Even when you think I am not there;

I bargain with you,
Whispering words of peace,
But I too become laden,
Amid seeming hopelessness,
Remaining the Hope of Glory!

The year is 2016. It started well and as the hands of time are rewound, I perhaps was at a comfortable place in my life having learned a few lessons along my career path about human beings not only in general, but at the workplace. I was about 33 years of age and due to turn 34 sometime in October. I was an English Teacher at a technical school that catered to students who opted specializing in learning a trade with some concentration on academics – the basics of course were English and Mathematics. I was also assigned to teach a course in Customer Service and Hospitality that was easy-breezy since I had a lot of experience in the fields. I enjoyed the time there because I was able to impact the lives of young people.

Every time I was met with some form of rebellion or ingratitude, I was certain to tell my students that a good education is important in such rapid times of change. Many took heed and could appreciate that the advice came directly from my heart. Others were not so receptive and this would dampen my spirit because there is no greater regret than having an educational opportunity and let it go down the drain. This is often realized later in life and you wind up dying to catch up if you are many of the unlucky ones. Defeating the odds is always rare and uncommon when you rebel young.

My seemingly bothersome appeal to students might have been of the divine. The turn of events which occurred at the end of summer, 2016, would set the pace for very uncertain times in Grand Bahama. It was already challenging since the rage of Hurricane Frances in 2004. Indeed.

Hurricanes are not friendly. Grand Bahama – the isle of my birth, is beautiful. It has so much potential. This northern island of The Bahamas is different from other islands within the country because there is a government within a government. The city of Freeport and Lucaya communities are under an authority and some laws differ for settlements outside of the Freeport-Lucaya jurisdiction.

The Freeport of my childhood was known as the Magic City and there remains a playful jealousy of Grand Bahamians by other Bahamians. Not the type of jealousy that causes hate, but a type of reputation through which you get that occasional comment in dialect, *"yinna' gattie be from Freeport – ya'll does carry on uppity"* (You've got be from Freeport. You act so boujee).

Grand Bahamians are different, but we do not believe we are better than anyone else. We simply live in the second city with boulevards and well-maintained areas. Our homes are farther apart, and we might not be so willing to know our neighbors.

On the Family Islands, inclusive of our Capital, Nassau, New Providence, people tend to be more social and the infrastructure in many communities might not be so well planned or manicured. I do not think it is a bad thing either. In fact, The Bahamas is a little paradise on Earth, and history dictates that countless travelers came to our shores to bask in island simplicity. The unspoiled and unplanned beauty of such a breathtaking paradise perhaps did not need all that planning anyway.

What is important to note is that Grand Bahama is the industrial sector of The Bahamas. Just perhaps that is why there is proper township-planning across the island. The vision of a very great man by the name of Lynden O. Pindling was the start of great things in The Bahamas. He was the first Prime Minister of the nation. During his legal studies in England, it was around a time when natives were not very pleased with being referred to as British subjects. At the time we were known as the Commonwealth of the Bahama Islands – not The Bahamas.

Likewise, with my personality I should like to think I would feel the same way if I were alive. Excuse me? Subject to whom, God? It most certainly could not be the Queen! But that is the way it was before July 10, 1973.

We were regarded as subjects and not British citizens. How debasing! We observed the Union Jack – we sang, *"God Save the Queen"* instead of *"God Save Us"*, and we spoke like the British, but were not given the same status as the British? I nearly went flat-line when a friend stated without apology that she felt that the British National Anthem is narcissistic. While I might agree, I do not think I will be so bold and not pay my respect where it is due.

After 1973, because of the effort and tenacity of Pindling, The Bahamas was born – *"The Islands of Shallow Waters and Coral Reef."* We, Bahamians, became the *"People of Shallow Waters and Coral Reef."* Granted I attended school in England and I now know why my environment is post-colonial in architecture, I am an extremely patriotic Bahamian. When I sing the National Anthem of The Bahamas, I get goose bumps. Who could not appreciate the lyrics penned by the late Timothy Gibson on our road to Bahamian Independence? They express:

"Lift up your head to the rising sun, Bahamaland;
March on to glory, your bright banners waving high.
See how the world marks the manner of your bearing!
Pledge to excel through love and unity.

Pressing onward, march together
to a common loftier goal;
Steady sunward, tho' the weather
hide the wide and treacherous shoal.

Lift up your head to the rising sun, Bahamaland,
'Til the road you've trod leads unto your God,
March on, Bahamaland!"

The words *"see how the world marks the manner of your bearing"* and *"'til the road you've trod leads unto your God"* are powerful! The world does know who we are, and The Bahamas observes the power of the Heavenly Father, as we encourage each other to do works in accordance with His will.

Shifting gears to Hurricane Matthew: it was a very terrible storm and was likened to Matthew, The Tax Collector mentioned in the Bible. And just like the people of the time hated having to pay taxes to Roman authorities, Bahamians were not happy with having to pay taxes to our authority for the consequent destruction likewise. I could remember that vengeful cyclone that passed with moderate speed ripping at the roof of our home. I could also recall praying that the roof would not be pulled off exposing us to the angry elements of nature.

Too, I remember my parents opening the front door just to get a breather. It was not over because we were directly in the eye of the storm. Bahamians know, having been raised in a hurricane belt, that if the eye passes over winds merely rotate in the opposite direction after the deceptive still of the hurricane.

As people peeped around the neighborhood from all vantage points, it revealed that a lot of damage was taking place and there was nothing anyone could do about it. It was Mother Nature at its finest; her debut on a grand stage

– she sang her song and led a tirade of a natural disaster. We would go in and endure the next half of the chaos to return to the destruction.

I could remember the downed trees and power lines. I saw the looks of people walking and driving with confused faces. I told daddy that someone's roof had flown into our back yard. No – seriously. Someone's entire roof landed in our backyard and its owner would eventually find it.

You probably felt that I spoke about the roof with such a casual tone. You are right – I did because in my lifetime, I have experienced far worse! You see back in 2004 during the aftermath of Hurricane Frances, never before had I seen the sheer and unbelievable evidence of force as I did when I visited a cousin's house. There I saw a "timber-fallen", evergreen pine tree in the living room. It was so frightening because the tree literally cut the large two-storey home in half. Thankfully, there was no loss of life and overall, across the nation, one death was reported because of a bad decision made. Apparently, the dead attempted to connect a generator during hurricane and unfortunately met his demise due to electrocution.

Sometimes there are strange deaths which occur as a result of poor judgment. One of the most common ones would be to swim in the ocean when rip currents are very real. Taking a drive through the city of Freeport was very depressing after Matthew. We knew back in 2004, among many other times of hurricane the great amount of loss that can be experienced. I remember passing a well-known church and it was as if it were converted to be featured in a

Sci-Fi thriller! The top of the church looked like there was a giant spider emerging but somehow it died in the process. Made of metal, it was dented downwards through the ceiling and the bent ends were forced upward. It was a sinister site.

When I returned to school to teach, I was left as disoriented as my students. Where was the school? It had actually been flattened to rubble. I was eventually laid off because there was very limited room to teach the young. Also, the school could no longer afford to pay all staffing, so teachers assumed more subjects than one specified area. Thus, a teacher who could teach several subjects was at an advantage and remained employed.

I joined the unemployment line with a mild acceptance of my fate. I did not have the time to sulk or entertain disappointment. I had to find a job soon. The newspaper I purchased one random day advertised job vacancies on a neighboring island called Bimini. It was an open call for applicants specifically affected by the Hurricane. Ironically, I was already dating someone from there and so if I got the job, it will have been an ideal move.

The day of the interview finally rolled around, and I joined a long line of hopefuls. It was surreal and honestly, I had never been in a situation like that before. I was simply confident and awaited my turn. I felt overdressed, but thankfully it worked in my favor. To the Human Resources panel, presentation meant everything. There were a few people ahead of me and from what I observed, there were persons whose resumes were accepted, but they were told that they will be called back later.

Yet, there were other persons whose resumes were received, and they were told to take a seat in another room. It was my turn next. I smiled and was chosen to be one of those candidates to go into the other room. There I waited for some time and I noticed that persons around me were dressed well and ready for the next step. We stayed seated for hours to the point we ordered a pizza and quietly entertained each other. It was such a group effort considering all that we were going through. Amidst the tragedy, humans – perfect strangers – have a way of comforting each other. The wait was so long, but we cheered each other on as we were called. The candidates on either side of me were applying for different departments so we kept each other motivated hoping for the absolute best.

Soon my name would be called and I went onto another room where tables were arranged to conduct interviews. My interviewer was already supplied with my resume because I had brought copies – another win for me. The gentleman began reviewing the resume and he started to ask brief, personal questions and slowly, as we built conversation, he was impressed. He was so taken back by, not only my accomplishments, but by my responses to his questions.

And then the question that won my position was to say something in Swedish and translate the meaning. I said my favorite quote in Swedish with a little bit extra, *"många bäckar små, blir en stor å. Jag är här för bättre. Jag heter Angelo. Hur kan man hjälpa?"* which means, *"many small brooks become a stream. I am here for better. I am Angelo. How can I help?"*

The whole point of using the proverb to my mind was that my potential employer, once a brook, will possibly afford me a waterfall of opportunity. It was enough for the interviewer to have told me to wait a moment to invite the Director of Rooms to the table. When the Director sat and perused the resume, he smiled and assured that he knew the perfect position for me. That is how I became an Executive Concierge which was the highest position in guest services at the hotel.

At this juncture, it is important to explain that the omniscience and the omnipresence of the Eternal Creator ties in beautifully by these series of events. God's presence can be like a hurricane. His authority impacts with the force of a natural disaster. His verdict in our favor as the Ruler over the universe is the grant of the rainbow at the end of the storm. His punishment is as harsh as those who lose everything – a shattered pride, to the extent of drowning, trauma, and inevitable loss of life. His voice can be heard as loudly as thunder. The hope He brings is as flashing-clear as the lightning across a raging sky. His passion can be felt in the falling of torrential rain. The blowing-howl of the wind reminds us of his movement throughout the Earth, here, there, and everywhere – His omnipresence! Yet, through it all, despite the damaging aftermath, He has the wisdom and power to bring us out of it smelling like roses – His omnipotence!

When I was told of my new role, I was further instructed to go and fill out my application to provide the necessary details to be housed in Bimini. I had a week to pack up my belongings and make all the necessary arrangements to relocate. When I arrived in Bimini, the process was smoother than I thought it would be. To my surprise, I was accommodated in a room all by myself. I did not have to share and that was the situation for my entire stay. I excelled in my new responsibility, and in retrospect, I was there for an entirely different reason and not necessarily for career advancement. There were a lot of personal discoveries learned through an initially blissful, romantic relationship that turned rocky and even toxic to an extent.

Furthermore, through all the good and bad that romance brings it molded the depth of my poetry and many pieces were birthed from an extreme form of love, sex and the unspeakable. I have no regrets because it all happened for a greater cause. I had learned the extremities of love and what you should and should not allow yourself to do or accept. I learned the importance of loving self before attempting to love someone else. One has got to love oneself until the love *"spilleth"* over.

I would leave Bimini sometime in 2017 for what seemed like a fast forward of time. Days went by so quickly because I was having the thrill of my life. I again relocated to Freeport for a short while due to another much milder hurricane that damaged the Executive Lounge in which I was stationed.

I entered another relationship in Nassau when I was employed at a very chic resort that was just as good and bad as other relationships. It was again very turbulent, but what

I learned, however, is how to avoid trickery in terms of romantic games people play. It has made me keener in love and, thus, there are no regrets. Why should we look to the past with regret when they are, but fleeting times of our lives meant to teach us valuable lessons?

Steady moments as they went, it is now the end of 2018 into 2019, and I wound up training for an entirely different position; a position that had been offered in Nassau before I left and so eagerly rejected. I trained for the new role nearly missing the mark but wound up doing pretty well on the practical end. I became a call agent. I appreciated the experience for what it was worth but became more interested in a training role. Besides, teaching is my background. Having received the requisite credentials I awaited the opportunity, but by fall of 2019, The Bahamas was targeted by Hurricane Dorian to impact the lives of Bahamians catastrophically!

In my poem, *"We Bury the Dead"* that was featured in the local Freeport newspaper in the aftermath, I narrate:

> An afflicted nation,
> Must bury the dead,
> In the blazing sun or rain;
>
> Foul, ripped flesh,
> The swarms of buzzing flies,
> After the deadliest of hurricanes;

Angelo D. Mortimer

On a scale so frightening,
The country's Treasury,
Could not save;

The thousands of souls,
Turned corpses,
Swept away to watery graves;

Because of him,
Dressed for destruction,
With a wicked, echoing name;

Dorian spewed massacre,
The Bahamas,
Would never be the same;

The survivors when it was all over,
Were blessed,
Or so it seemed;

Broken to tears,
For the dead and chaos,
Wishing to wake from the awful dream;

Dorian hovered over the north,
For days and nights,
Just prowling;

The more he fussed,
So the brave would fear,
Winds of wolves were heard howling;

Abaco is flattened,
Then Eastern Grand Bahama,
Throughout surrounding cays;

As Haitians are guzzled,
Of Pigeon Pea, the Mudd,
And whoever in raging seas;

His torrential tears,
And secret tides,
Would maliciously flood the Earth;

Roofs flew off,
Homes crumbled by force,
Sending most into rising dirt;

It was a disaster,
People were scared as hell,
By the news that terrify;

Of the unlucky clinging to anything,
To be washed away,
And die;

Succumbing to Mother Nature,
Either trampled to death,
Or drowned;

Vanished in the aftermath,
Dead for weeks,
And still not found;

Angelo D. Mortimer

Dorian had no mercy,
Parents and children,
Lose your breath!

Whole families,
Simply wiped away,
By the ugly sting of death;

The smell of sewer,
Overtook the air,
As the fallen decayed and rot;

Their bodies,
Crushed in ruble,
Slowly bloating until they 'plopped;'

There was a time,
You could hear Bahamians,
Always complaining for something;

With tables turned,
We quickly learned,
To be grateful for almost nothing;

Overwhelmed with grief and panic,
On the verge,
Of losing our minds;

One day to be,
On top of the world,
Finding life to be unkind;

Now faced,
To stay or move away,
And many moved away;

Leaving country,
Because there was nothing left,
To rebuild day by day;

Indeed we the survivors,
Our strong resilience,
Is louder than drowning screams;

We were shattered,
A people battered,
Rising despite extremes;

Out of the grave,
Where sorrow reigns,
And the grieving bury the dead;

Such memories fading,
Into the flames of the sun,
How bright are the days ahead!

The events which unfolded were of course very frightening. I had never experienced something so traumatic in my life. The fortunate thing is that the area in which I resided at the time the hurricane hit my island was not in the direct path of Dorian. I decided to weather the storm with my parents at their home.

The master bedroom was designated as the safest location in the house and so we huddled together. We were convinced things were not looking pretty good outside when conditions deteriorated. We could hear the wind howl like a teapot whistling to a boil on a stove with the urgency that it might explode if not turned off right away. The sounds were of heavy rainfall with a combination of anything no-matter-the-weight being thrown around by force in different directions.

Because it was so dark outside, we were blinded from seeing any danger that might be headed toward us. The rising tide, a falling tree, and elements of nature and/or man-made missiles are examples because neighbors failed to secure their property properly.

It felt like our roof could be compromised and lift off at any point. It was not the familiar train track noise that demanded prayer during Hurricane Matthew. It was, rather, the seemingly deliberate attempt of the monster outside to open a can of tuna like a starving young man with his bare hands.

Moreover, one thing that we did which I believe helped to reduce wind damage was to keep the windows open under the plywood that covered the windows to protect them. This allowed the air to flow freely as opposed to causing a pressure field in the house to burst the roof off.

I remember lying down on the ground of the carpeted master bedroom and listening intently to the prayer offered by mommy as my eyes were drawing closed. The warrior was at work and somehow the peace of God was so surreal. It was so peaceful that it lulled me to sleep. I can only recall getting up during intervals when the roof was being pulled upward just a pull too strong and feeling like I should wait a few more moments to ensure my view of the ceiling would not change suddenly to a roaring image of sky. I was not scared as many are when surviving a category 5 hurricane.

    I felt helpless, though, because the battery-operated radio provided coverage of the weather conditions outside and reports of people crying out to be rescued and fearing for their lives. Additionally, there were people panicking as they described that there was water coming into homes unable to tell that it was the ocean about to swallow them whole. The ones who were not drowned by their own homes made it out alive either temporarily or with the fighting chance to survive sharks swimming in the streets. The Atlantic Ocean decided to swell and rise bringing anything inland with it. Indeed recovered corpses revealed the terror on people's faces, some with locked screams and clear-struggle to breathe.

    When it was all over I could sense deep inside that it would not be the same for years to come. I sensed the harsh reality because I could feel and smell death. I could almost hear the unheard cries of the trapped-presence lurking of the soon-to-be-forgotten spirits that roamed the Earth. It was a tragedy that has never hit the country before that moment – the hour of unwelcome destruction that I knew only to happen in a movie had come. This reckless vehicle towing a painful aftermath moved at the core of The Bahamas. It shook us collectively and the northern shores of the archipelago have still not quite stopped weeping.

The storm has happened some time ago that can be counted by the years that will certainly follow. But the timeless message is that I now understand why in the midst of unrest mommy lifted her voice to the heavens on that near-doomed night with such authority. I now understand the power of prayer, and the fact that a sincere appeal sent up can move mountains to summons showers of protection and blessings.

It is because there is a Creator above who knows us by every strand of hair on our heads or those lost. He can hear our voices and by our very cries and appeals, He has the power to dispatch His angels and other hosts of the invisible realm to encamp around and save souls from the strongest pull into darkness.

Our Almighty Father in Zion is accessible and we can be granted what we request of Him. The only things He does not provide are things that are not to be provided at the time. This can be for many reasons including, but not limited to, those things that might be fatal to us, physically or spiritually. A responsible mother or father is not going to feed babies solid food if it will choke them to death.

As it has been shared prior, I am a proponent of destiny. As our omniscient – most all-knowing Creator, He is aware of the choices that keep us farthest from our purpose and fulfilling our destiny. His omnipotence gives Him the unlimited authority to keep us on our path. Often, we allow our stubbornness to get the best of us and we wind up suffering and hurting ourselves because we want to live our best lives according to our own goals.

When conscientious decision is made to set up our lives without the guidance of God, it is like teenagers moving out of their parents' home and not seeking their blessings or any form of advice for the outside world. This does not mean that the child will fail, but what is undeniable, however, is that the child is more likely than not going to arrive to a more successful path if relying on the wise counsel of parents or any adult, for that matter, who has been on Earth for a longer time rather than self.

A person who has had to endure hardship, unnecessarily, from an adult stance after years of maturity usually does experience regret by their willing refusal to take advice from the wise. Indeed, every single adult is not wise, but every version counts. By all records of fact starting from the very foundation of time, whether they are the accounts of people before us or those of us individually, we know that there must be a being out there that possesses a power beyond human comprehension, as that supreme source is the giver of our very own intelligence. We know that we exist, and it is only logical that the very first Creator knows we are here and our future that will unfold.

Furthermore, there have been very remarkable times in our lives when we could have died physically, mentally, spiritually, or emotionally, but a miracle manifested through a method or a message that remains unexplained. Without a shadow of a doubt – Our Creator, or whatever we conceive Him to be, is *omnipotent, omniscient, and omnipresent*. By virtue of the fact that we are individuals – with individual mindsets, tending and trending to agree and disagree on the very appearance of God, suggests that one of the major reasons we coexist is that we seek the many faces of our complex-simple God.

CHAPTER EIGHT
Affirming the Most High

Inspired by singer Osinachi Okoro or 'Sinach' in her song, *"Waymaker"*:

God illuminates the path.
Such a Doer of Miracles!
True to His promises,
He is the bright in the dark!
Our God,
That is who He is.

And inspired by the song, *"He Lives in You"* from, *Lion King*.

The Creator is in you,
Like He is in me,
He protects creation,
Everything that be,
Into a ocean,
Declaring truth!
That He dwells in me,
Just as He dwells in you.

The clues of our Creator's existence are all around us. He is certainly, *"The Bright in the Dark,"* and *"Exists through You and Me."* Allow me to make it clear that I am a Christian with simply an extended view of the world. I believe The Universal Creator existed from the original void – He is the light in the darkness but was never of it.

I call that Creator God among many other names used to describe His indescribable nature. I am convinced, wholeheartedly, that God is *'triune'* or three in one and has created life as we know it. My understanding of *'triune'* is God reigns in a Supreme power in Eternity, He has manifested and continues to manifest throughout mankind, *"One"* of whom is Jesus Christ, and He remains attached to us through His being a *"Comforter"* since human beings are part spirit.

I reason that God was and still is spirit and He chose to experience life physically. Thus, He sent His Son, Christ Jesus through Immaculate Conception by way of the Virgin Mary to be His very own physical embodiment. Denying this possibility is saying God cannot do anything.

I believe that Jesus Christ was raised to take on the sins of the world and was destined to be ridiculed, persecuted, and crucified as the Perfect Sacrifice – the Lamb of God.

I believe in the death and resurrection of Christ Jesus. He died on the first day and arose on the third, whereby the strict Law of Moses had been done away with and we are saved by His grace once we, the Christian, believe in Him.

However, I believe Christianity is one of many subscriptions which connect to God. Thus, I or anyone else on the face of the Earth, are not in the position to judge another subscriber's path to salvation.

I believe in the Law of Moses, the Ten Commandments, which was uttered through the Voice of God:

- Thou shalt have no other gods before me.
- Thou shalt not make unto thee any graven image, or any likeness of anything that is in heaven above, or that is in the Earth beneath, or that is in the water under the Earth.
- Thou shalt not bow down thyself to them, nor serve them: for I the Lord thy God am a jealous God.
- Thou shalt not take the name of the Lord thy God in vain; for the Lord will not hold him guiltless that taketh his name in vain.
- Remember the Sabbath day, to keep it holy.
- Honour thy father and thy mother: that thy days may be long upon the land which the Lord thy God giveth thee.
- Thou shalt not kill.
- Thou shalt not commit adultery.
- Thou shalt not steal.
- Thou shalt not covet thy neighbor's house [anything in it].

On the basis that the world is saved by grace from the Christian perspective is the understanding that Christ Jesus is one of God's many manifestations in the flesh, which was able to endure life as a human to grant a more holistic understanding of human strife and create laws which are more livable. This is the Hope of Glory because mankind has been spared of a very course law and can press toward the Mark of the High calling that is in Christ Jesus.

Finally, I believe in the Holy Spirit – the Comforter that connects me and anyone else who is open to the Holy Source – the Universal Creator. This belief is the core of my faith and should be respected. The God of Christianity encourages love, which became the Greatest Commandment.

Abba, our Father, lives in Zion. God is one Creator – He is the great I Am that I Am, "Ehyeh asher Ehyeh;" the King of kings and the Lord of lords – the God of Abraham, Isaac and Jacob. I worship with the Jews when they call out to Elohim "The God" and Yahweh "The Living God." God is Adonai "My Master", El Shaddai "My Supplier", the Messiah "The Messenger", The Son of God" and Logos "The Word."

In unity, I call Him Jehovah, as do the Jehovah's Witness meaning "Our Lord" further shortened to "Jah" affirmed by the Rastafarians. God has been and forevermore be *El* and *Jehovah*:

Jireh – "My Provider"
Rafi, Rofa - "My Healer"
Nisse - "My Banner"
Mekodishkem, Makadesh - "My Sanctifier"
Tsuri, Sal'l - "My Rock"
Shalom - "My Peace"
'Roi - "My Shepherd"
Uzzi, Gibhor, Eyaluth - "My Strength"
Sabaoth - "My Protector"
Magin - "My Shield"

Shammah - "My Friend"
Tsidkenu - "My Lord of Righteousness"
Kadosh - "The Holy One"
Emeth - "My Truth"
Elyon - "Most-High God'
Olam- "Everlasting God"
Berith - "My God of the Covenant"
Peleh Yo'etz - "My Wonderful Counselor"
Esh Oklah - "All Consuming Fire"
Moshiah - "My Savior"
Mikkarov - "My God that is there"
Tsaba - "My Lord of Hosts"
Abir- "My God, the Mighty One"
Tsaddiq - "My God, the Righteous One"
Hashopet, Shaphat - "My Judge"
Palet - "My Deliverer"
Gaol - "My Redeemer"
Bashamayim- "My God in Heaven"
Immeka - "The God with You"
Mauzzi - "My Fortress"
Menusi, Makhsi - "My Refuge"
Gemuwal - "My God of Recompense"
Chasdi - "My God of Good and Purity"
Quanna - "My God is Jealous"

Blessed be the seven (7) names of God per the tetragrammaton: *El, Elohim, Eloah, Elohai, El Shaddai, Tsevaot Jah* or *Yah* has also been added to the original tetragrammaton.

God is our Advocate – the Almighty. He is the *Alpha* and *Omega*, meaning the *Beginning* and the *End*. This makes the Creator the Author and Finisher of our Fate, the Bishop of Souls and Bread of Life. He is a Friend of Sinners and the Desire of Nations; God is the Light of the World – "Jah Goyim" – The Lion of the Tribe of Judah and the Bright Morning Star. God is the Rock of Ages and the Ancient of Days. The Rose of Sharon, He is the Judge of judges, and remains the Father of the fatherless and Mother of the Motherless. God is everything of authority and wondrously.

Just as I embarked on a journey to discover some of the additional names of God within Christianity and Judaism, I learned that there are 4,300 religions of the world in the year 2020, according to Adherents, an independent, non-religious organization. The major religions include:

- Confucianism
- Taoism
- Buddhism
- Hinduism
- Jainism
- Sikhism
- Bábism or Bahai
- Christianity
- Druze
- Islam under Shia, Sunni or Sufism
- Judaism
- Rastafarianism
- Zoroastrianism
- Black Hebrew Israelites

Further research illuminated why the region of my birth has been influenced by African tradition. The Transatlantic Slave Trade forced distinctly civilized nations to accept another form of religion. I am proudly a citizen of the African Diaspora and most familiar with the claims that forms of spirituality that were brought to the west is witchcraft.

Batuque, Candomblé, Haitian Voodoo or Vodou, Kumina, Macumba, Mami Wata, Obeah, Oyotunji, Palo, Ifa, Hudu, Quimbanda, Santería (Lukumi) and Umbanda bear the faces of God, yet they wear masks of taboo. They are the hidden faces because the beautified faces of the west, perhaps most ugly, made others feel unworthy, hideous, and inferior.

I maintain an alternative point of view. I believe that the abovementioned faces of spirituality are no less valid than the more accepted religions but offer a truth to who God is. I find it rather presumptuous that the believers of any religion can esteem themselves as high as to suggest that their understanding is so superior to that of another. Religious texts in their purest form promote love.

I can agree that there are many more religions throughout the world much too numerous to include at this juncture. The reason I refer to African religions, in particular, is because they are most relatable to me. Also, it births a love for who I am that does not foster trying to get rid of a part of me. It is the part of me that is as mysterious as the color black. Racial elements of Black, Jewish, and Hispanic electrify my bloodline. Yet, being black is your soul attacked; being white ain't always right and being

Hispanic is just dramatic! However, collectively, I am beautiful.

Here is a thought: had the West Africans been left alone, for example, and not enslaved, would that mean they were not connected to the Source – the Universal Creator? It must be borne in mind that their religions do not suggest their way as the only path to God – but Christianity, for example, would claim that Christ Jesus is the way and the light and only belief in Him would grant everlasting life.

This is the basic premise of Christianity, correct? Does this suggest that all persons who do not know of Christ Jesus have never seen or could never see the Face of God? Is it being suggested that God is so narrow a path and shy? He is quite capable of introducing Himself if needed. Yet, He will not force Himself onto His creation. God does not need us; we need Him.

CHAPTER NINE
The Thing about Organized Religion

"For there is no difference between the Jew and the Greek: for the same Lord over all is rich unto all that call upon him. For whosoever shall call upon the name of the Lord shall be saved."
Romans 10: 12-13

It is common to consider others strange when they do not immediately observe personal belief. It follows that it must be a lot harder to embrace difference and attempt to reach some form of understanding. I have long been convinced that religion divides people more than it unifies us.

Interestingly, religious teachings are not necessarily the problem. It is often the people who follow them, which lead to discord. More often than not religion makes *"us" right* and *"them" wrong* when the human race, collectively, is trying to understand a Universal Creator – One Source.

Faith is exactly that – "faith" and not "fact." Faith can be defined as a degree of individual truth, but fact is undeniable truth. Some might ask me why my faith in God is so real to me. It is because I look to nature and realize that there are some things that mankind could not do when I apply sound reasoning. Then I turn to the accounts of the Bible, which I must say are not entirely accurate, but a lot of it is and stands out like a tower.

While I proclaim that God is my Creator and Christ Jesus is the Messiah – the Savior who extends the Hope of

Glory, there are many things within the walls of Christianity that I greatly dislike. I express some in a poem I wrote called, *"That See-Do Religion."*

>Back in the islands,
>Where I was raised,
>It is the Sunday ritual,
>To tithe, to praise;
>
>The See-Do religion,
>Like the taboo,
>Some do,
>Casts spells on the masses;
>Making spiritual leaders,
>Holier than thou;
>
>It transforms their words to be Gospel,
>By the Voodoo they do,
>Causing the unimpressed,
>To lift an eyebrow;
>
>And while the Good Book,
>Declares we study,
>To show ourselves approved,
>Our fragile, holy creed;
>
>We dare,
>Denounce other faiths,
>When many,
>Dare not read!

Angelo D. Mortimer

Our See-Do religion,
Apparently leads to salvation,
Saving souls,
From sin and abomination;

It seduces the sway of torsos,
Stretched arms and waving hands,
To an unseen God,
Way up in Zion,
A Holy fellowship,
The proverbial iron sharpening iron;

We walk into churches,
Pious and upright,
Call it uptight!
Or In a Meringue dance,
To be filled of the Holy Spirit,
And possessed by a drunken trance;

It is certain you would hear us,
Shouting Amen and Hallelujahs,
Loud and passionate enough,
To awaken the dead,
From death's sleep;

And curious children,
Would mimic to learn,
… They peep …
To rehearse;

The actions of the sanctified,
Convincing enough,
To escape,
Any generational curse;

We are conditioned,
And positioned,
To declare one understanding correct,
Forming bias,
Against anything else,
An oath of disrespect;

That the conviction,
Within another denomination,
Judge another religion,
Is merely contradiction!

Perhaps it is right,
To say that this manipulated mindset,
Of a people so God-gung ho, yet kind,
Reap the bliss of ignorance,
Within the shackles of their own mind;

To think we tithe,
Such an unnecessary tradition,
Of the Old Testament past,
Even if we give our last;

The ancient trick,
Is the prick,
Of guilty conscience of congregations,
As slimy as Eve's appeal to Adam;

Against sound reasoning,
We are trained,
To steal our own savings,
Meant for when it rained;

We carry our offerings as sacrifices to the altar,
For repetitive sermons,
Sensationalized,
A freak show at a circus,
The more you give,
The more hype the hocus pocus;

So is tithing above or below 10%,
Valued to be less?
Since outstanding faith is immeasurable,
And passes the test?

Refer to the Good Book,
Read the Lesson of the widow's mite,
She actually gave 100%
Her unshakable faith by Jesus was declared right;

Thus, with tithing,
It burdens a potentially cheerful giver,
And forsakes the very ones,
For whom it is meant to deliver;

I deliberately take it there,
Shall we explore?
Why are the leaders of God becoming so rich?
And the poor remaining so poor?

Angelo D. Mortimer

Where are the soup kitchens?
For the hungry to eat?
Why are the people of God,
Not preaching in the street?

Instead See-Do leaders make cheerleaders,
Turning their affections on prophesied possessions,
Only to maintain,
The buildings in which we meet!

I came to know,
Worship is two or more gathered,
Among other truth,
As my soul keeps crying;

To agree with sacred Bob Marley-lyrics,
"His feeling to bomb a church,
Because now he knows,
That the Preacher is lying";

The Holy Ghost,
Needs no invitation,
Neither lavish church nor cathedral,
To feel appreciation!

It moves as a fragrance,
Throughout the atmosphere,
Be it far, near,
And everywhere;
The anointing it brings,
Does not discriminate,
Among the rich or poor,
She participates;

Angelo D. Mortimer

Her message spreads love,
She does not shun,
Like a blazing fire,
Within everyone;

Its smoke should attract,
The most immoral to the fore,
Like prostitutes, the homosexuals,
Alcoholics, atheistic-intellectuals,
Calling them to the fore!
Fornicators, gamblers,
Backsliding procrastinators,
But it's Christian judgment,
That keeps them outside the door!

And what is worse,
Many leave church empty,
This defeats the point!
The Holy Spirit came in His precious name,
But spirits were not joint!

Countless, revered See-Do leaders,
Have fallen from grace,
Meaning each word they preach,
Hawks as spit to Jehovah's face;

Untouched souls exit church doors,
Returning to old sinful ways,
Yet moments ago,
There was a thrill of praise;

The point of spirituality,
Is answering, "Why"?
Why fight to live?
When we are living to die?

And so there is nothing,
More tragic than the ole' time religion,
When the soul is grounded,
As a flightless pigeon;

It is hoped this disconnect,
The truth will mend,
A hellish fallacy,
To the heavenly end;

And See-Do believers will awaken,
With the sight of eagles,
Flying high where spirits roam,
To die as eagles,
To fly away to the truth unknown –

If a child is raised believing that a certain teaching is the only and true path to salvation, then it will be very difficult to believe otherwise. I am blessed to have had parents who are Christian but raised me to be open and read about other cultures for a bigger outlook. I was encouraged from very early in my life to explore, question and express how I felt.

In a society where the instruction of the day is that children are to be seen and not heard did not settle well with mommy, in particular, because she believed that children are capable of intelligent thought and, collectively, everyone can learn from one another.

As citizens of a world enriched by diversity, we can seek to coexist by simply allowing ourselves to accept that we are all entitled to individual truth. My truth is true to me. Your truth is true to you. If our truths differ, it is not left to me to say that my truth is correct over yours because the Creator remains unseen. Our faith in the invisible is equally powerful and can only be proven by what cannot be manifested physically. Thus, the construct of our faith need no mutual agreement, but we deserve mutual respect. That is all. Consider the following scenarios:

"The Chit-Chat with Cecilee."

The conversation went something like this: Angelo, *"Very recently I walked into a popular bookstore and ordered a novel entitled Satanic Verses by Salman Rushdie. The young woman at the counter peered curiously at me from over her spectacles then asked, "You're not from here, eh?" in the carefully articulated lingo Bahamians tend to reserve for tourists or those a bit hard of hearing. When I responded that I was born and bred in Nassau, and indeed very much "from here" all vestiges of politeness dripped off her face like molten wax. She blinked at me once, then twice; then took off her glasses as if this new perspective would assist her in what she obviously considered utter madness. After a long and strained silence, she asked me if I belonged to some type of "cult" and if I would like to "know the Lord."*

At that point I was squawking, because knowing Cecilee's elegantly-sarcastic nature, it could only go left from that point. I was so angry Angelo. *"Struggling to maintain both a straight face and my patience, I simply asked if she could be so kind as to place my order, hand me a receipt for my deposit and, if she was still up to it, have a nice day. She did all three with such sullen hostility that I seriously doubted that my last request held any veracity,"* conveyed Cecilee to my very interested soul.

When I attended college in Nassau before relocating to England for further legal studies, I befriended Cecilee more affectionately called "CeJay." She was the friend that taught me the word "eclectic" as that is precisely how she would describe herself and unashamedly so.

I appreciated our friendship from the start because of her personality and strong command of the English Language. You could always count on CeJay to learn something new and exciting since conversations were always fresh and current.

One day we had met up, and by then we had both advanced to Intermediate Collegiate English. CeJay was upset about what she deemed to be "religious intolerance" in The Bahamas and stated that an upcoming graded paper would be a perfect opportunity to address it.

CeJay and I were instructed by our English Lecturer to write an informal argument to which she wrote, *"Damned to Hell."* Having described the event to me, I told her that she should include her experience that happened all too often in our very Christian society. She scored an 'A' overall for the paper and it had been published in the University's bank of outstanding essays. Her report, thus, will be referred to again further down having obtained CeJay's permission which we have discussed time and time again.

"The Passionate Convert"

Call him "Nameless." I would rather he remained that way. And this is not because we aren't on speaking terms, but rather we have not spoken in a good while. I would rather respect his privacy. I met Nameless shortly after I started University in England. He had recently converted to Islam from Christianity and was keen on getting me to convert. He managed to get a mutual friend to do so and I presume he imagined that the same would happen in my case. This is not to say that his points were not valid as to why I should become Muslim, but an incorrect approach in ministry is that your viewpoint should never be seen to be superior to that of another.

Burnt orange to one person can be dark orange to someone else. Who is wrong when debatably they look almost the same? This causes undue conflict.

In CeJay's, "Damned to Hell," she writes, *"Webster's Dictionary defines religion as a personal set or institutionalized system of religious attitudes and arguably the key word is 'personal' ... I do not want some pious stranger knocking at my door to minister to my presumably lacking soul. The very term 'personal' denotes something that should be kept very close to one's person."*

In the case of Nameless and I, he was like a pious stranger knocking at my door to minister to my presumably lacking soul. Clearly his newfound religion gained him a celestial star in heaven and I was to be pitied. The point remains that Nameless' conversion to Islam presented a new set of beliefs which is simply unconfirmed truth. Had

Christianity been the confirmed truth, there would be no conversion.

Every religion, therefore, exposes some degree of light. An appropriate quote mummy taught me is *"A person convinced against his will is of the same opinion still."* The fact that I am still a Christian is a testament that at the time Islam was proposed, my conversion was not meant to be nor was it ever.

"The Uncomfortable Dinner Conversation."

Back in university, she became an amazing friend. Now she is my only godson's mother. Her name is Nouria and, to date, she calls a spade a spade. In The Bahamas you might hear a native say, *"Her mout' is her problem and she don't slap up, slap up."* That is our way of saying Nouria is forthright – she speaks her mind with few, if any, words – period.

Nouria and I were excited about meeting two Hindu sisters at a University restaurant to sample the food students were raving about. It was there that we engaged in a very friendly conversation with the sisters until we touched the topic of Hinduism. The sisters so proudly spoke about Varna which is a caste system that classifies people within the religion. The four classes, they explained, are the Brahmins [priestly people], the Kshatriyas or Rajanyas [rulers, administrators, and warriors], the Vaishyas [artisans, merchants, tradesmen, and farmers], and Shrudas [laborers]. Varna included a fifth group being the lowest of the caste composed of tribal people and the "untouchables."

I was prepared to accept the information as a cultural difference, but Nouria was not so passive. The fact that the Hindu sisters were not directly from India was the cause for Nouria's disgust. The bombshell question posed was, *"Being a young black woman and based on your understanding of the caste system, what am I; an untouchable?"*

Seconds began to feel like an eternity, but finally one of the sisters tried to justify that the caste system had a collective function through which members of each caste worked together for a common good.

What fueled Nouria's fury was the very word *"untouchable"* and with each attempt made to justify this arguably unfair system was my gradual wish that the ground could swallow me. Nouria's points, being fiery and bold in nature, were in no way rude, but extremely direct.

In retrospect, I avoided the issue because I did not want to call out the injustice. I did not want to hurt feelings. This attitude changes nothing and classes such atrocity to be a "cultural difference" so it becomes the norm and nothing changes. Because the Hindu sisters were in fact Kenyan, it showed that religious traditions and convictions are sometimes held against sound whispers of morality, justice, and common sense.

It might be observed that this scenario is similar to that involving "Nameless." Yet, it must be made very clear that there is a difference between assertively attempting to convert persons to another religion as opposed to gaining clarity about another religion. I believe that through peaceful discussions, not only will people be able to learn, but it will either promote change of religion or further strengthens one's faith. Everyone on Earth is entitled to their individual understanding of the Creator. And from the flow of scenarios that have been shared, it is accurate to conclude that human beings are all on a path toward a holistic understanding of life.

For most of us, we've realized that we did not just wind up on Earth for the sake of it. We were all put here to carry out a specific mission in fulfillment of individually, divine purpose. In so doing, whether we want to embrace the theory or not, we merely live, to execute our roles guided by the Creator of all religions. Then, in the spiritual totality of things, when we die, we merely take off our robes. This transition grants access to another reality where those of us who are left have never before experienced.

CHAPTER TEN
The Most-High Above all Religions

"… Many people cannot fathom the concept of religious freedom because of their immovable conviction that their religion is the only "right" religion in the world … non-Christians are scorned, hated, feared or pitied, as if this character flaw has become the downfall of the individual's life."

Cecilee "CeJay" Hilton, from her essay, *"Damned to Hell."*

Excuse my diary approach to this chapter, but I write on a special day. Today is September 5th, 2020, and the time is 1:47 p.m. Eastern Standard Time. It is exactly one month before my 38th birthday, and I find this day particularly special because mere hours ago I completed chapters 8 and 9 of this book. Those chapters presented a challenge because I somehow experienced a type of 'writer's block' for about two weeks.

In the meantime, however, I had discussions with awesome friends who encouraged me to keep writing since I told them about my dilemma. Earlier in the morning, I stumbled across a status update on WhatsApp from a good friend, Alyssa, who broadly opened up my mind. It was around 11:40 a.m. that I saw a meme that resonated so much with how I feel about religion.

I responded to the meme then gave her call and it lasted for some fifty-four minutes and fifty-eight seconds on her reply text of the word, **"synchronicity."** Indeed, it was a case of *"alignment"* or *"perfect timing"* since the best time is the Lord's time. Very often we might find that our tasks in life are harder when we try to do them on a human schedule as opposed to allowing the Lord to guide our steps. I call it a case of synchronicity because I had been feeling very passionately about some points on which I will elaborate in a moment.

But firstly, I will address the abovementioned quote that started this chapter in terms of its definition of religious freedom. Earlier CeJay suggested that Christians are inflexible when it comes to doctrines that are outside Christianity. However, this specific quote being referenced starts with the words, *"many people"* since this attitude is not only common among Christians. This attitude includes members of religions around the world. It is a flaw and certainly not the way forward.

Let us look to the heart of the matter. As a Christian, biblical text encourages us to study to show ourselves approved unto God. The word "study" does not necessarily mean that we must study the Bible to be approved. The very fact that God is a God of diversity suggests that we study all we can to be approved. This means that we can learn from many sources.

Think about it. Would you not agree that comparing many sources is better than the study of one source? For example, say a candidate who is trying to get a job: would it not be better for the candidate to be well rounded? Experience and certification are a plus. A person who has merely studied, possessing a degree does not qualify over a person who possesses the same degree with additional experience – impossible!

So why have followers of religion become so gung ho that they are correct to the exclusion of all others? Is not religion faith versus truth? A person's truth is not general truth. It is true to the believer. Certainly evaluation of all perceived truth solidifies one's faith by the art of deduction. In simpler terms, if I say all cows are fat, Joseph says cows are plump, and Mary says cows are heavy, which is truth? Could it be that all mean the same thing or is religion as good as an entitled opinion? Opinion is certainly not fact!

I propose that as human beings we ought to be mindful that the Most-High has created a world of diversity. No person under the sun has the right to sit in the seat of judgment and condemn anyone else of a different faith. How dare anyone place God or whatever we perceive Him to be in a box! His infinitely powerful nature cannot be contained to human understanding. He is inconceivably inconceivable! It is believed that every religion paints a Face of God – the Universal Creator. He is that He is.

I am sure that many of my Christian brothers and sisters will think that I have taken this discussion to a borderline blasphemous level. That is fine. I do not apologize, for even the Bible warns that I shalt not lie – I should like to think this includes speaking my "truth."

For example, during Kindergarten, I schooled in a predominantly black school in a predominantly black country. From grade three, I moved to a "mixed" school of students. Understand my predicament. A young black boy christened in the Anglican denomination that depicts a white Jesus. Indeed, I learned that I was made in the image and likeness of God – the "triune" God. Thus – Jesus was white according to the portrait I grew accustomed to seeing throughout Christian homes.

From young, I recognized no resemblance. Although I was "Sunday-ritually" attending mass, pressed and dressed, neither did I understand that the image I reflected was spiritual – my spirit, nor was I taught that I, in fact, resembled Jesus Christ physically as outlined in the Book of Revelations who is deemed to be colored in appearance.

Having read and being educated of this fact, who then do whites and everyone else resemble? Therefore, further research revealed even more profound answers which often require that we investigate outside the conventions of the religion that is taught.

Many truths remain hidden within Christianity just as they are hidden in other religions. Furthermore, when religion is incorrectly applied, it keeps humanity caged. I was caged personally by the portrait of Jesus and watching countless movies starring actors of surprisingly different races. I was also starved by the "affliction of omission." By this I mean many religious leaders are content with selective, agenda-biased and feel-good sermons.

That is not how it should be because even Christ Jesus did His best to ensure that the most common of commoners would receive His teachings. He hung out with the lowliest of the lowliest. He used both direct and indirect methods which required thought and careful consideration.

Most noticeable was Jesus' unforced policy of encouraging His followers to enlighten themselves to miraculous discovery.

I find that especially in my region of the world, masses of congregations rely on God-called-pastors versus the True and Living God for revelation of His word. Many of us are too lazy to read and do the required research; yet we rely on the interpretation of a leader who is capable of misinterpretation.

If you have intelligence, you can also interpret and discuss for the correct meaning. One is allowed to think for oneself. I can agree with Karl Marx's claim that *"Religion is the opiate of the people."* This does not only target my Christian brothers and sisters, but all religiously one-sided citizens of the world.

Religious one-sidedness fosters a type of ignorance. CeJay explained in her essay,

> *"… It is this very same attitude that has marred the history of Christianity for centuries and given the religion itself a very carnivorous reputation. From as far back as the Middle Ages when the Christian Crusades slaughtered thousands, to the Inquisitions authorized by King James, from the witch hunt craze in America and Britain, to the situation still festering in Northern Ireland between the Catholics and Protestants, Christianity has had its share of blood on its hands. But let's not just look at Christianity. There are wars between different sects of Islam, there are religious skirmishes erupting endlessly between the various tribes in Africa (for example, the Hutus and Tutses) and just about every religion known to man has had its share of blood and human suffering. Yet most religions are based on peace and love. So it cannot be the fault of the various gods, or even the ideals on which each*

religion is based, but rather the ignorance of men using religion as an awful mask to hide both ignorance and intolerance."

The jail of religion is very similar to the imprisonment of slavery. "His Story" – the history that man tells is a version of "the story." History has been watered down to make reading comfortable.

For example, the tale of the black slave will not be felt the same way by a white person as a black person. Empathy is not reality, but rather a connector to emotion. A person imagining what someone else is going through is weak compared to the person actually experiencing the injustice. Only he who feels it knows it.

Blushes of red on white high school student faces that day in history lesson, crept onto little black high school student faces remaining invisible because blacks were not created with the pigment to simply blush.

I came to understand that as a race, Blacks must escape the chains of our minds due to ancestral oppression deeply rooted in our DNA. We were originally innocent, yet traps which promote the *"Black Crab Syndrome"* have been set up by society's "order-of-the day" depending on the region of our births. Slavery is supposedly abolished but many remain enslaved in their own mind. We are who we think we are.

The underlying demon that sits in the shadows screams we are worthless making puppets of racists who see we are powerful beyond measure. Think about it. Don't all humans, regardless of race, want to strip power of anything that makes us afraid? Say a grizzly bear approaches on a mission to attack, granted blacks are *"monsters,"* wouldn't you take a rifle out to shoot it down? Indeed.

Appropriately, and spilling over into my University story in England was another enlightenment – that **"ah-ha"** moment, on the issue of "good hair." And it was not based on the comedy, *"Good Hair"* starred Chris Rock years before. A mutual friend of Nouria and me commented that I had "good hair." The comment arose because we were heading out to the town center but had limited time to get dressed. So our friend felt that because his hair was coarse and mine was soft and curlier, that it would take more time for him to get ready. That was the ideal moment for Nouria to chime in that she never wanted to hear him say something so stupid again.

It was her contention that there is no such thing as good hair, but that the grade of human hair varies from thin to thick, and all hair is made of the same material. Nouria so conveniently supported her view by drawing particular reference to Queen Nefertiti of Egypt. It was Nouria's claim that what appeared to be a tall hat upon Queen Nefertiti's head was in fact her hair. She further explained that a coarser grade of hair was symbolic of good health, longevity and prosperity while softer hair was generally valued as a sign of weakness.

My spirit raged like a windstorm in that moment because it is well known in the black community that our parents and parents before welcome the births of loved ones in firm rebuke against heads of knotty hair – the straighter the hair, the better. Nouria encouraged that we ought to read more about our African lineage and not be so brainwashed by the West – Ouch!

Bringing the focus back onto the topic of the validity of religions, Nouria's unwavering **"African-ess"** – that sense of *"African self"*, empowered me as it was taught back in high school that Caribbean people among others form a part of the African Diaspora. Put a simpler way, as a result of slavery, the word, **"Diaspora"** speaks to the *"uprooted movement"* of people throughout the world.

So here is a thought. Based on the Christian claim that the only way to the Father is through the Son Jesus Christ, and additionally, considering the fact that long before the enslavement of African peoples, they had their own form of spirituality, is it safe to say that those dead tribes of Africans before knowing Jesus are currently swimming in the Lake of Fire?

But was it not Christianity the religion of the conqueror most if not all the time? Who, then, is really of the Lake of Fire to wallow in it? It does not make sense that a God who has created us all – would sentence His own creation to hell for failure to observe one version of His indescribable nature.

The commandment "Thou shalt not steal or kill" is as loud as "Thou shalt worship no other gods before me." To think that the slaves were forced to deny the only God or gods they knew is quite unfair to say the least. Stripped of their spirituality, and brought to the Caribbean, for example, a large fraction of the slaves were from West

Africa. When one does research, one will discover perspectives unchartered and the unsaid.

As I studied more, I began to understand my ancestors who were spiritual practitioners with powerful rituals and belief in bush spirits among other things through:

- The *Akan* in Ghana and Ivory Coast,
- The *Dahomean Mythology* in Benin and Togo,
- The *Efik* in Nigeria,
- The *Edo* in Benin Kingdom and Nigeria,
- The *Hausa* in Benin, Burkina Faso, Cameroon, Côte d'Ivoire, Ghana, Niger, Nigeria and Togo,
- The *Odinani* and Yoruba in Nigeria,
- The *Serer* in Senegal, Gambia and Mauritania,
- The *West African Vodun* in Ghana, Benin, Togo and Nigeria,
- The *Dogon* in Mali, and,
- The *Vodun* in Benin.

Such research began to support beliefs I held near and dear to me for many years. Indeed there is a degree of truth in all religions and people who subscribe to those outside Christianity could not simply be said to have never been linked to the Source and inevitably sentenced to hell.

Then like lightning the word *"Omnism"* flashed before my eyes. In that moment when I read the meaning of Omnism, it was as if I could finally breathe – I could exhale since there was a school of thought that actually would help me to explain what needs to be said as best as I can.

"Wow", I thought. It took the year 2020 to usher in the understanding so 20/20. The random meme flashing on a friend's WhatsApp status defined that "Omnism" is, *"The belief that no religion is truth. The truth is found in them all."* Of course this made me very curious and so I did some online research which pointed out that the earliest usage of the term, "Omnism" was in 1839 by an English Poet by the name of Philip J. Bailey.

Similarly, I was guided to read a little about the Bahá'í faith which steered me to a more collective appreciation of world religions. Bahá'ís will tell you that God is singular and all powerful, but through the passage of time, religions evolved through Manifestations of God who happen to be the founders of each religion. It is the vision of Bahá'ís that the world will be unified which fosters prosperity of all nations across races, classes and creeds.

Thus, in closing, I believe that depending on the region of the world where persons are born dictates the religion to which people will be joined. I believe that God, our Creator, judges according to a person's demonstration of love and kindness throughout that individual's lifetime. Religions, I propose, are merely systems that advise to live a lifestyle that is pleasing to the eyes of our diverse God.

CHAPTER ELEVEN
My Spiritual Journey

Every time I observe human beings, I witness the handiwork of God. It is amazing how He carefully crafted each of our bodies to withstand the passage of time. All of us are individuals with distinct features that are imperfectly perfect. We have been distinctly molded to suit and fulfill our divine purpose. But to think that our bodies are simply physical is a huge misconception – a deception even. And so we need not get into an unnecessarily deep discussion about the dynamics of how we function other than to say that we are both flesh – our dying self – as well as soul and spirit – the part of us that never dies. Indeed! A part of us dies and a part of us will live forever.

This theme is common across religious divides. To arrive at a very concrete conclusion that we are partly a spiritual being requires the simple example of falling asleep. When we are tired, our bodies will follow a ritual that is learned. We go to our beds because our animated selves are our very walking corpses. And if we can see ourselves in this light we would see that our physical bodies should not be so celebrated.

Further, we will come to understand why vanity through the mirror is considered offensive to our Creator. Certainly, there is nothing wrong with being confident in the evidence that we are wondrously made, but it is another thing to be arrogant.

It is certain that there are fellow human beings that appear blemish-free, but this does not give them the right to esteem themselves above the outwardly blemished. In fact, the real blemish is a flaw of the inner man. There is nothing scratched-record about being focused on inner beauty versus outer beauty. In fact one who is rich in spirit might seem unattractive at first, but inner beauty will outshine.

So back to the example of falling asleep: it is clear that the body is weaker than spirit. When we close our eyes, I should like to believe that it is not as simple as a fleshy brain being responsible for our existence and should it cease to function, we merely cease to exist. We cease to exist, only physically, if the brain stops functioning. The stronger proof is the power of dreams. Why do we dream? Science tells us that it is due to *"Rapid Eye Movement"* – cute.

I do not dispute that the eyes move rapidly during the dreaming process, I just believe it is a little more than that. I propose that just perhaps the eyes begin to search for soul and spirit. There are the Dreamers and the Prophets – people who awake with a glimpse of a future occurrence or a specific message. Oftentimes people forget what in fact they dreamed about. Why does this happen so consistently? Could it be that many dreams are forgotten because our spirits experience another realm daily? And within that realm are realities all the more frightening which expose mysteries that we simply cannot handle?

It is perhaps valid Einstein's theory that, *"energy cannot be created or destroyed. It can only be changed from one form to another."* Might I propose that even energy could not exist without a source – perhaps the source is the Creator Himself – a spirit of "simply is." Additionally, I believe that the spirit that exists in us is simply energy that is linked to that original source.

Very recently my cousin died and it was interesting how I began to see how very fleeting life could be. We worked together for several years in the Timeshare Industry and when I left the industry, I would see him every so often and then, not so occasionally. A few years passed whereby I would eventually learn the very sad news that he had died.

But what stands out in my memory was the sermon presented by the Pastor at his funeral. Very eloquently he shared many points that were simple. Of the many ideas that he discussed, a few moved me to apply to my own life. He spoke about the importance of time, that we should value it, living each moment in the present. Emphasis was made on how many of us are stuck in the past and we often worry about the future – how true that is!

Secondly, the congregation was charged to use time doing what pleases God – the Creator, as only those things will last.

Following was the flow into the topic of humanity and how we as people should live in love and unity.

Additionally, because life is short and precious, the Pastor encouraged that we say to loved ones that they are indeed loved as we greet each other on Earth. He continued that we ought to give people their flowers when they are alive. It makes no sense to express love when they cannot appreciate it.

Lastly his point that money and material gain could not be carried beyond the grave made a strong impact. His reference to Alexander the Great was a brilliant example. He explained that even such a powerful man requested that when he died that his arms with hands wide open be extended outside his casket to symbolize that despite his wealth and many conquests, he could take nothing with him. Indeed this is true.

The sermon in its entirety had taught me that the sting of death is like the flow of lava burning everything in sight. Every day souls travel to the Land of the Dead when life for some in the Land of the Living is not so forgiving. Those who are left behind must endure the dim of tears in the moonlight, too often, pleading for the sunrise.

A few chapters ago, I mentioned that I have a gift of seeing visions of future events and important messages to deliver. I elaborate at this juncture by sharing an experience that involved a friend's mother who had died. To this day, I am amazed by how strong that close friend was during her time of grief. While she did not have the best relationship with her mother during our childhood, my friend developed a more loving one closer to the time that her mother would transition to a better place.

It was a slow death because the health of the dearly departed gradually failed. However, my cousin's death was sudden and unexpected. The experience was quite different and more celebratory when my friend's mother died than to lose a cousin or anyone close in a global pandemic. What stood out was a revelation that was given to me. I am tickled slightly because persons who are found to hear or see things the way that I do are deemed crazy. But I can assure you that I am farthest from that.

At the gravesite after all the weeping, time passed as people began to get up from their seats to leave. The way fate would teach me a spiritual lesson is that everyone left and I was alone with the undertakers who began to finalize the burial by closing the grave. And to myself I asked the Creator through my thoughts, *"You mean to tell me that they are just going to leave her here?"*

I was 37 years of age at that time, and it was not the first funeral that I had ever attended. The question I believe was not one that my reality demanded to know since the answer is quite the obvious. Why exactly does the graveside exist? The answer was given through familiar utterance which always sounded like a terrifying yet soothing voice all in one.

I heard, *"the flesh is dirty and unclean. The grave is where the flesh and spirit separates on Earth to be free as the heavens."* This revelation pushed me closer to the brink of understanding my spiritual walk all the more. It was because I thought to myself. It was the confirmation that flesh is so foul that even our loved ones, composed of flesh, will come to scorn us, just as they will leave us in our graves. That did it for me.

Furthermore, it confirms the powerful reality that just as we are born alone, we, too, must die alone. Such a spiritual awakening led me to fully understand that I need no validation from a fellow human being, but the validation of the One who has created me, distinct from you and anyone else.

Essentially, we are part physical and part spirit-beings, and I contend that the spiritual realm of human interaction is most electrifying. When we meet each other our vibration – or the connection – is either shallow or deep. The physical interaction is when we exchange basic pleasantries.

It is getting to know each other with the understandable wall we build because everyone does not deserve to know us intimately. It is the random, "hi how are you", and the conventional response, "I am fine, how are you", when we both could be dying inside.

Superficiality causes the soul to enter empty bonds instead of genuine friendships which expose toxic ties since no one cares to recognize if there is really nothing in common. Equally emerges the pretense that you are in a loving and successful relationship when there is no reciprocity – no equal give and take – no equal yolk. So you wind up in *"situationships"* that became bad situations you could only dream of escaping for more reasons than one.

Sometimes I find myself saying that the average human being is very pretentious and superficial because the fact is many of us are merely existing and not living. If we ask ourselves the question, *"Am I really living"* our answers might surprise or even scare us. There is a difference between one who sleeps and one who is "woke." The body rarely sleeps when the spirit is woke. The body gets tired, not the spirit.

The blessed and more meaningful connections are unforgettable. Challenge yourself by rewinding the hands of time to an occasion where you met someone and you simply clicked with the person – and with ease. As you engaged in conversation for about twenty minutes you felt like you knew them for a long time to the point you confess *"I feel like I have known you forever."* Maybe you have; from a previous lifetime. Who can disprove beyond a shadow of a doubt that the soul of a man is not timeless.

Many of us are so caught up in the idea of an afterlife. Here is an invitation to ponder the question: was there ever a "before-life"? I recall both hearing and reading a scripture when God told the Prophet Jeremiah that He knew him before forming him in his mother's womb. Is this suggesting he had a soul before or that he was merely given life at the point of birth? Jeremiah was appointed to be a Prophet, thus, I perceive that we, as human beings, are born and appointed to a purpose long before we actually exist leading to the theory of destiny.

As a Christian, I can assure you that many of my fellow believers would not think that far because just perhaps there is the remote possibility that reincarnation is quite real. Remember Christianity is the way forward, hallelujah? How dare I entertain another "faith" – another "point of view" – that challenges "one's truth" to the exclusion of all others!

Pardon me, but what I am getting at is simple. Faith is faith. It is personal truth within the ambit of one religion versus another. And so it is suggested that faith is not necessarily the pure, unadulterated truth. It is not the universal and shining light and can be challenged so long as it has not been proven to be fact.

Progressively, discoveries stirred within me a hunger to challenge all that I have been taught. I seek a more profound spiritual understanding. I am evolving to understand the validity of spirit being energy and that time granted by the Creator is a gift. Thus, this encourages me as I encourage you to be mindful of how you spend your time. Our energy, taking into consideration that there is not so much time, should guide us in the knowledge that we must protect our energy. The more energy we exhaust on people or things which are negative is a path to destruction.

Our time is a gift so those who we give our time to must be identified as appreciating it. The things to which we devote our time are incapable of telling us whether they are good are bad. We must identify and control if we will or will not entertain them. Mastery of the Art of Time Management is the skill of the successful human. We must seek to budget time and master discernment.

It is often said that one cannot give one's best from an empty vessel. Former talk show host, Oprah Winfrey expressed it wonderfully, *"Fill your cup up; surround yourself with people who fill you up so that your cup runneth over."*

Notice she did not say fill others up until their cups runneth over. If you did, their cups will overflow to others.

What about you? By this answer is the discovery that spiritual growth demands *"self-fullness."* It is okay to be selfish sometimes, but just not all the time. We must willfully choose to be with ourselves using time to shape our lives. Meditation is essential, and rest is, too. These are the keys to inner peace.

I had a very enlightening conversation with a Buddhist recently. We talked about many topics through which I was able to learn things I never knew before. The discussion turned to spirituality and we both began to uncover that we were both raised in the Anglican Church, but that my findings are in line with non-religious Buddhism.

His knowledge of science was mind-blowing. But I shared what we mutually found unshakeable. It was agreed that science relies on proof to explain the world around us. Yet, spirituality relies on faith – the things that remain unseen and further unexplained.

So I posed that one of my gifts is to dream and even hear "a familiar voice" that speaks of things that will happen in the future. Such events are about situations that will arise that I could not know based on my own intelligence. They unfold just as I described however long it takes thereafter.

I told him that if a person disproves what I know I saw or heard that the person is calling me a liar. Also, evidence of an oracle or prophecy comes to play when predicted events actually happen. The things I dream – the things I see – the things I hear – they actually do materialize. So they become material fact like science.

His response when asked how science explains this was his understanding of Quantum Physics that could not go very far into explaining exactly how I come to know these events. Again, I am not alone in this world. There are many persons gifted with this ability so I am not special, but rather, the gift is.

For example, we are the Seers, the Prophets and Shamans to name a few within the religious context. The occult "apparently" extends to witches, warlocks, wizards and sorcerers, which require an entirely different book. It is an area, quite frankly, to which I do not particularly care to subscribe. While it was no debate for an overall prize, my Buddhist buddy confessed an outright block concluding that science can only attempt to explain the already seen.

Speaking of Quantum Physics, I stumbled across a meme that shared, *"Quantum physics tells us that nothing that is observed is unaffected by the observer. That statement, from science holds an enormous and powerful insight. It means that everyone sees a different truth because everyone is creating what they see."*

Indeed, this is very powerful. So when I see a vision with open eyes that appears like a daydream, is it not my sight of the actual world around me? Dare you question my imagination? If to you or anyone else, my gift of sight is my imagination, how can it be if the actual events occur and I am able to introduce the people who will attest that these things happened? I do not know the persons to whom I deliver a message. So how is it, logically, do I have a genuine interest in changing their paths I know nothing about?

Even further, who is the teller or revealer of such events if my intelligence cannot be responsible? I firmly stand on the belief that the Source is the Creator or any chosen communicator from His world – a place we cannot see. That place I have come to know as the spirit realm.

A more intimate understanding does not set me apart or make me better than anyone else. In fact I really do not look for, or expect any credit. However, life becomes all the more worth living. Spiritually, it encourages me to search for answers as opposed to simply accepting what has been taught.

Indeed, interpretations are as good as opinions. Interpretations are also subject to error and personal bias and are not always reliable. What is well founded is spiritual food eaten by self. Eating the spiritual food from others is like babies eating the chewed food from their mothers. It would taste so much better when you eat from your own plate of food.

Therefore, your truth is your truth and my truth is my truth, as we respect the individual truth of others. We are deserving and entitled to our truth that is free from criticism in a collective effort of peaceful coexistence here on Earth. What my spiritual journey has taught me is that we are not here by mistake or merely trying to make sense of it. It can be further clarified. We are here in pursuit of purpose.

CHAPTER TWELVE
The Creator – A Spirit

Within Christianity, "I am that I am" are some of the most holy and infinitely-defining words of our Creator. And we, human beings, are created in His image and likeness. So it follows that because God is unquestionably who He says He is, God created us to exist and to declare that we are that we are.

Thus, the powerful and universal question is, *"who is it that we claim we are to arrive at the conclusion that we are that we are"*? This leads to a deeper question: *"how; how can we even suggest that we are that we are when our points of view differ with respect to exactly how we arrive at that conclusion"*?

Distinguished by religion or lack thereof, the question pierces more: *"where did we find the grounded evidence to support our individual truth"*? Lastly, *"what makes us so sure, beyond a reasonable doubt, that we are correct"*?

Call Him Singular or Plural – The Lord of Hosts, Our Creator is One Source! He made us all. We need not argue about The God of Many Faces because He cannot be argued. He is simply the Beginning and the End. He is of the mysterious and indescribable void; yet, He is not of the darkness being the Supreme God of Light. God is above the gods, demigods and other deities across religious interpretation. He is the First and the Last, the King of kings and Lord of lords capitalized above all manner of mortal appointments. He is simply the Most-High! He is Yahweh

– our Elohim – the Creator above all creators and creative comprising "the him", "the her" and "the it"!

In the Good Book, God instructs His creation to worship Him in Spirit and in Truth. He is the same God who instructs us to study to show ourselves approved. I speak about the Intangible Creator – a being that remains and will eternally remain unseen until we take on the embodiment that can withstand His power and majesty. Such mega-intelligence cannot be perceived by physical eyes or human theory – simple!

What is required of us for even the most remote understanding is to firmly acknowledge and accept the unseen powers that be and not so confidently turn a blind eye like they do not exist. Such knowledge is retrieved within the ambit of faith and meditation. It goes deeper than the mind's eye to the place where our conscience and moral compass resides – the part of us that already knows that there is God.

For example, basic intelligence across humanity identifies that there is some superpower responsible for designing the world around us. There is evidence of mysteries that cannot be explained by basic reasoning. Thus, it is shallow to accept that we merely wound up here on Earth to merely exist without meaning or purpose in the world. And so to discover our purpose distinguishes who "exists" from who is "living."

It is expected and more natural to be perplexed about supernatural entities of a supernatural world. That is because flesh and everything associated with it are tied to a natural world and cannot be used to grasp the elements of a supernatural world.

When I think of God, I think of energy – the first energy – the first potential and the first kinetic forms. Potential energy in science is energy that just exists as it holds the power to move and be transferred becoming kinetic or "moving energy."

So within the context of mega-intelligence, think of God in the beginning as "divine sleep." And just as we dream as human beings, the Creator originally slept as He envisioned the Creation that inexplicably materialized through a divine process that is said to be over a period of seven days. Versions of this phenomenon vary; yet, whatever we, as humans conceive, them to be, the essential point is we are here. It is beyond baffling to explain without solid proof which version is correct.

The unshakeable fact once again is that we were born of a womb through the contract of childbirth by way of a natural mother. We know that our natural father held the seed that was planted just as the first seed was held by Adam and received by Eve. We know that it must be along this storyline as it takes a man and a woman to produce natural life.

How then do we communicate to the Creator? While the nature of God is very challenging to explain, it is actually less challenging when it comes to how we spend time with God. I seek to elaborate on five words – the channels through which I communicate with the Father of Creation: focus, silence, meditate, pray and worship. However, I must say that what works for me might not work for you because we are all different.

First, I focus. Focus is a very powerful skill and is needed to prepare for what exactly God seeks to do or say. The world is a very noisy and distracting place. Oftentimes it is not even our fault. Everything under the sun was made to fulfill purpose even if it was designed to distract you.

In The Bahamas, for example, there is a very annoying bird and to date I have never quite figured out what bird it is. Every morning that creature caws a melody that seems to start at a high upbeat eventually falling to a low note in a kind of sadness. It sounds retarded. The very fact that the bird annoys me is already a distraction because the time I take feeling annoyed, I could be getting on with my day. Yet, the bird can be seen as God's way of starting my morning from a spiritual standpoint; it depends how we see it.

The point I am making is anything can distract us and in order to get the attention of the Creator and hear His response requires concentration on God and only God. We have got to spiritually tune in becoming deaf to everything around us. Approach His throne with full intent because He has too many children rampant in the Earth for anyone of us to believe that He should beg for our attention.

Tune in every way possible – physically, mentally, emotionally and even intellectually – intellectually, insomuch, as knowing that your spirit man must connect with His spirit in order to communicate. This is the level of spiritual engagement that is needed and can be achieved through discipline.

It will happen as surely as when the lights go off into that temporary blindness you feel when everything seems dark. Then gradually you become one with the darkness and your sight is regained correct? This new vision, which composes newer shades of black and gray, is likened to the place where you experience Abba – Our Heavenly Creator.

Secondly, when we focus we achieve silence. We arrive to the domain of inner peace where we open the portal of our soul and spirit to receive spiritual blessings and meaning. It is in the still and quiet that we can reach the space in which the Creator freely roams. This peaceful place is the necessary connection where it all happens. It will occur even though you are still connected to the physical world. But the process initiates a heightened consciousness to be encouraged, guided and energized. There is no other feeling like it.

Thirdly, meditate. Meditation is such a beautiful thing. When one has achieved that inner peace and silence, there is nothing better than basking in it – simply meditate. Think positively and reflect. Now when you reflect, do not do it with effort. Simply let your spirit send the images – dream. Allow your mind to journey to periods of time whether you wind up spiritually in the past, the present or an unfamiliar place, the latter of which could be a snapshot of your future.

Breathe and relax. I perceive that when the Creator allows you to see those images in your mind's eye, He is allowing you to see how He perceives you. If positive feelings are derived from this preview then they are times during your life for which you should remain grateful. If negative feelings are derived from the images, they are perhaps areas of your life that you should seek to improve.

Your thoughts which are heard and not uttered are heard by God. Talk to Him – share your thoughts about the good and the bad. It is during these times that it is as simple as asking and immediately being given the answer. Sometimes, though, I have found that I might not get the answer during a specific interaction, but somehow the Creator creates an encounter whereby someone might say or do something in passing which clearly provides the answer.

God is not boring. He is genius. He finds appropriate ways of teaching us. The lesson will leave us speechless because His points are always delicately carried out through good and bad experiences. His influence is profound. It is during meditation that we can appeal for the many signs and wonders of the Most-High.

Next is prayer. Prayer is one of the most communicative tools of the human mammal. It is how we approach God in the conviction that He is almighty and that His verdict is perfect when it comes to our lives. Because He is the King of kings, we are royalty. He deserves that we come to Him with both thanksgiving as well as our deepest fears. When we feel like life is too good to be true we should pray. When we feel like life is not worth living and that we feel He has forgotten us, we should pray. We should pray without fear of punishment especially when we pour out our concerns in truth.

Our Creator is awesome and always resolves any form of appeal on time. I have witnessed prayer removing mountains, literally and figuratively. I have seen the haughty fall and the meek rise as a consequence of prayer. Sometimes the results seem unfair, but when God judges a thing it is fair. He sees and He knows everything. With and without warning, He renders the verdict.

Lastly, engage God in worship. Worship Him with all your heart, mind, soul and might. Indeed He is worthy. All of us were given talents and gifts. Give them back in worship. If you are a speaker, lift your words without embarrassment and praise Him openly. If you must do it quietly – do so. If your situation allows you to speak aloud – preach and cry out your Hallelujah.

If you are a Singer, sing your songs in alto, tenor or soprano. Your voice was not created to hum and hide – it was designed to renew the souls of creation. The same goes for the Musicians – make a joyful noise that resounds in the Earth!

If you are a Dancer – use your body as an instrument to paint the Creator's grace and majesty. If you are a Writer, express your text to uplift humanity by the way you lock your words. Whoever you are, worship by virtue of who you are in the name of divine purpose.

Earlier I will have mentioned that the Creator is omnipotent, omniscient and omnipresent. He was likened to electricity and His movement described as "electric; near, there and through the air." It supports my theory that God can be compared to energy, as He is a wondrous and powerful being. He remains unseen, yet He existed from the foundation of time. His presence can alter any atmosphere to be overcast with a mist that mesmerizes as blinding fog. His cloud-cover appearance can emerge at any time, as our Creator is also the Master and Keeper of Time. He is the Source of the past, present and future generations and His reach spans back in time throughout eternity. In His world, time is fluid and so He sees and knows everything about His creation.

Have you ever gone to an environment and was complimented about how awesome you made a perfect stranger feel? Were you ever told on a separate occasion by other individuals that they feel like they have known you for years? I have. I have been told by many, *"I just love your energy"!* This impression cannot be solely based on the body alone. People react explosively to an explosive spirit. Impressions formed in a physical world are derived from the movement of body through a collective network of physio-emotional processes which define our personalities.

In simpler words, the spirit is so huge, the body can only submit. Since God is a spirit, it is indeed correct to worship Him to the best of our abilities in spirit and in truth – that is, we must praise with our all, convicted that God is worthy of the praise. We praise Him because He is Truth; He is the Beginning and the End – The Marvelous Creator.

CHAPTER THIRTEEN
Agape – A Love like No Other

Looking back through my mind's eye, I understand more and more why I like music so much. I can remember sitting in the front, passenger seat of mommy's gray Nissan Cedric hearing soulful music played aloud. I was about eight years old. Even if I wanted to resist the passion of the songs, it was practically impossible to do so. I would sing Julio Iglesias,' *"My Love" and* feel every lyric. And at the end mommy would let me take it away with words that claim that, *"World love, is world people."*

To mommy's credit, surrounding me with these types of vibrations fostered my respect for humanity from a very tender age. Childhood memories of Miami bridges on those many visits from The Bahamas stand out. I could remember the homeless and the suffering. I could remember that I was a very compassionate child. I would cry for mommy and daddy to give them money. Granting my wish, they would hand me American one and five dollar bills, and as our rental car slowed down in the poorer areas, I would give random people money. I had a huge heart and could sense their thanks because what I gave was probably all they had at that moment. In return they would say, *"God bless this little boy."* I could feel their hopelessness and developed a strong sense of empathy for others.

As I grew older I learned to control my kindness so it would not cause heartache. Of course this was sharpened after many years of people taking advantage of my good nature. Forgive the flashback in time, but there is relevance; the relevance of a child's love. The love expressed by a child is often innocent. It tends to be shared in its purest state, and excludes all manner of condition.

However, love can be tainted. Love when uttered in the English language becomes less fragile because we have been socially conditioned that it is the expected thing to say. People say the word very casually, yet love is not a shallow emotion. The use of the word love has become as deceptive as when a perfect stranger asks, *"How are you"* and while you might be dying inside you fix a fake smile and respond, *"I am fine and you"?* The sentiment behind the words, *"I love you"* should be reserved for when we truly mean it since it is both a sacred and crowning emotion.

Opponents might suggest that the use of the word love should be understood within context. Nonetheless, I believe that the use of the word, altogether, should be avoided and replaced with the word *"like"* or *"appreciate."*

For instance, when I moved to Sweden back in 2000, I found out that Swedes are very specific when they express love to one another. The verb älska – "to love" is expressed to people for whom there is genuine love beyond basic familiarity or association. Acquaintances would be addressed using the verb gilla – "to like or appreciate" and the verb, längta (efter) – "to adore" would be used to address a significant other extending to marriage. The word "älska" can be used between lovers as well.

There are no contextual inferences that can be drawn in Swedish; you say what you mean and mean what you say with a clear boundary established in terms of who is who in one's life.

When I returned home from Sweden and people asked me how Swedes are as a people, I would always describe them as being very reserved. They might appear very timid at first, oftentimes staring sheepishly, because inwardly they are intrigued by strangers. Yet, they are not inclined to befriend perfect strangers so easily. Indeed strangers remain strangers because it is uncommon that Swedes will start a conversation with you unless they had a little too much to drink.

What I often appreciated about this cultural observation is that Swedes either really like you or they really do not. They very rarely flatter showing you exactly the way they feel by their choice of words, too. There is no gray area. You are either respected because humans are minimally deserving of it or you are loved – point blank!

Particularly interesting to me during my education was when I attended the now University of The Bahamas (UB) and was required to take a religious studies elective in pursuit of my Associates Degree. I absolutely enjoyed the lecture on the types of love, as I was wide awake at that class. I can remember my note taking almost word-for-word because the topic truly captured my attention. Interestingly, there are eight types of love in Greek:

- Philia – close friendship or brotherly love.
- Pragma – practical or logical love.
- Storge – familial or instinctual love.

- Eros – erotic and intimate love.
- Ludus – playful and uncommitted love.
- Mania – obsessive love.
- Philautia – self-love.
- Agape – unconditional and selfless love.

When it comes to the love of the Creator – He is the epitome of Agape. Besides, He created love and is the endless supply of it. Unconditional love means God loves us regardless of our race, nationality, creed, political persuasion or sexual orientation. Could this really be challenged since we know that the Most-High has created us all?

Selflessness entails loving beyond any form of what is personally believed to be the proper way of loving. It involves spreading love through self-validity having already learned to "love self" to a state of "self-fullness." In the context of the divine, the Creator must have created it, and thus Agape emanates from the very core of His being.

I would take it further to suggest that Agape incorporates every form of love. Our Creator, through the passage of time, has shown through all accounts that He can be:

A brother and a friend since, across religious divides, the Creator and His messengers, like Adam, King David and many more, have demonstrated friendly relationship – *philios*.

He is practical and logical in that laws, like the Ten Commandments, were created which govern how human beings should conduct themselves among one another – *pragma*.

God is the divine father and mother since spirit is genderless; we are children of the universe. He openly displays His love in more ways than one. To think that the Most-High carefully designed this world for all to appreciate and enjoy speaks to His love and care for us.

Additionally, it touches on His clear concern about our sustained well-being as He created the continuity of time to learn and evolve. He exemplifies parenthood – *storge*.

He is the husband or bride. Within Christianity, for example, the Creator initiated companionship through the first man and woman. For us to conceive the concept of marriage, God must have known it well before the very foundation of life. Being the Father of Creation, God created all living things with the ability to procreate through intimate love. Another Christian observation is the birth of Christ Jesus through Immaculate Conception that shows that He is the Divine Patriarch – *Eros*.

God is a humorous friend and confidant. The Creator has an awesome sense of humor. You can tell by His creation. Have you ever seen a hairless cat or a blowfish? You need to be able to laugh at yourself and be funny all at once to think of such funny creatures. While we cannot see the Most-High, we can sense that He is truly the Author and Finisher of Fate. He allows events to occur whether good or bad to express His many sides. That is why we can experience humor now and again sometimes feeling like the Creator went through great lengths to prove His point – *Ludus*.

The Lord can be a territorial friend. Christianity describes God as "jealous." This is not the same as the evil emotion from which human beings suffer. It is jealousy in the sense that He is jealous enough to allow us to encounter challenges so we will not forget that He is Creator and is needed. He is jealous enough to seek revenge in the name of justice when human beings believe they are more powerful than He is, and in turn, believe that they are unbreakable without His help. He is jealous in the sense that He is protective of our well-being. Call it obsessive or even possessive, the Creator deserves our full attention, yet still grants us the gift of free will – *Mania*.

Jehovah loves independently. Have you ever been in a relationship with someone and enjoyed the luxury of having your own space to evolve? It is the same when it comes to the Most-High. While God might not be immediately present, His affection is felt.

Biblically, it is said that our Heavenly Father does not share His glory. That touches on His invisible nature. It is like a husband who occupies His home office most of the time and his wife freely roams the rest of the house and the world on trips He pays for to be enjoyed with and without Him. God built the heavens fully staffing it and the Earth, likewise.

As the Creator is the Master of Time, He is here, there and everywhere. He is able to spend time to Himself basking in the universal worship of His Majesty spanning the planet. Because He has made us all, we praise Him uniquely and He receives and expresses His gratitude in just as distinctive ways. As the Creator gives to us, His attention, He, too, takes it away. The God of Many Faces, Jehovah, the King of kings, can be selfish through *Philautia* and selfish through Agape.

Just as we marry each other throughout the human race exchanging vows at the altar, the Creator's love surpasses natural vows. His extreme love is unconditional. He is faithful and loyal beyond any possible offence that is forgivable. The love of a mother for her child is perhaps the closest to it – not the love of a woman who merely gives birth and fails to nurture her young, but a mother, the woman who loves her newborn beyond measure through infinity and beyond.

God is *Agape* and a God of Second Chances. He forgives us no matter how grave we perceive our sins to be or how immorally unattractive we seem to society. God forgives us with the degree of love with which He expects us to love each other even when we opt to despise or judge.

Very recently I read the words of St. Teresa of Avila who expressed in a poem, "Christ Has No Body" (1515–1582),

"Christ has no body but yours,
No hands, no feet on Earth but yours,
Yours are the eyes with which he looks
Compassion on this world,
Yours are the feet with which he walks to do good,
Yours are the hands, with which he blesses all the world.

Yours are the hands, yours are the feet,
Yours are the eyes, you are his body."

In this context, Christ represents the Spirit of the Creator. In an earlier chapter, I mentioned that we, human beings, are triads or "three-part": body, soul and spirit. The body is self-explanatory, yet the soul and spirit tend to be the parts of us that are not so easily understood.

Very simply, the soul is our intelligence and the part of us that allows us to live and endure the human experience. It is our conscience, the sound of our voices and incorporates our five senses: hearing, seeing, tasting, touching and smelling. Thus, the soul is linked to our bodies.

The most essential part of us is our spirit. It is the link to our Creator and the supernatural realm composed of divine hosts. Without the spirit, we will be lost on Earth with no grounded sense of belonging. There would be a hellish loneliness felt. One only needs to imagine the pain of an orphan to perceive the immense torture it is to be disconnected from the Most-High – Eternal Mother and Father in one.

This leads to a very good question, that is, how do we determine or calculate time spent with our Maker? The easiest way to explain this is by the reintroduction of the words omnipotent, omniscient and omnipresent. Humanity survives in the present, which is a period of measured time. God lives in the Land of Forever: He continuously survived, survives and will survive. Because we possess a spirit in a body, we experience our Creator in quantities of time through events which occur. Our bodies, souls and spirits are merely accessed at the same time and we express our feelings of life.

God, being spirit, can show up at any time possessing whomever He pleases throughout humanity at any given time. This is because of the spirit in us which grants Him the spiritual authority to access our hearts and mind. However, this only happens when we are open to being imbued by His Majesty. The Creator, however, possesses us by force if He needs our attention. Otherwise, we have been granted free will. His presence can affect us by what we feel through emotions. Depending on His reason for the encounter, we can feel extreme joy to terror.

There are the mysteries of the Almighty – those with which we need not trouble ourselves. We hear stories with respect to the unimaginable – miraculous stories of people returning from the dead – such seeming fantasy and fables of zombies and many more mortifying events that are unspeakable. Upon closer investigation, just perhaps they are quite real.

The ironic thing is spirituality remains a very uncomfortable discussion. It might be taboo – yet taboo is possibly another name of the Creator. Because a notion appears far-fetched does not negate that the notion is real. The central philosophy of world religions simply adds to the totality of the Universal Giver of Life. Points of view are meant to serve as points of view.

Theories of our Creator are understandably conditioned by our culture, environments and upbringing. Peaceful discourse should be welcome. The depths of spirituality can truly blow the mind, but so does the nature of the Most-High. Again, what resonates is that there will be attributes which baffle when it comes to The God of Many Faces.

CHAPTER FOURTEEN
Most Benevolent and Merciful

My most loving and dearly departed, Aunt Val, died in a fatal limousine crash in 1996. She was a gorgeous woman. She was the same woman who named me Angelo; the same woman who would coddle me when my own mother could not express her maternal affection soon enough due to Post-Partum Depression; the same woman who always seemed to stand out time and time again; the same woman who, to me, epitomized womanhood and graceful femininity.

Aunt Val was an Entrepreneur who lived her life like a true Leo. She was born one August first, and seemed to shine in purpose – travelling to far ends of the Earth because she often said, *"life is a bitch, then you die."* Interestingly enough, I have matured to believe her words since the world is a noisy place in which we, as human beings, must bask in the good or evil or even a bit of both until the day "thy kingdom comes." My fond memories of her guided me through the years because she taught me the value of living one's best life.

1996 would be a year that I would learn the first lesson of the dangers of attachment. I will never forget the day she paid a surprise visit to Freeport dressed in a white tuxedo. She was far from a show-off, but she looked like a celebrity.

It was the year that I was not as spoiled as I may have thought I was by her. It was the first time Aunt Val was not so much on my side. I remember I was going through a difficult time at school with students and Aunt Val would be a source of strength to me. I told her everything just like I would tell mommy. Incredibly Aunt Val gave me some very sound advice that reshaped my thinking for a change. It was simply that, *"there comes a time in your life when you've got to face your own problems, Angelo."*

    I was about 13 and her words birthed an awakening in me that took stock years later because it is so true. I could recall going to my final banquet with Aunt Val and her winning the grand prize that evening because she was sitting on the winning chair. I could remember her radiance and beauty turning heads that Sunday at Christ the King Anglican Church. I could remember that call that she had died mere weeks later in Trinidad. It was the unexpected sting of death of which no one wants to learn. It was in that moment I felt that all my aunts died because without her, what was the point of even attaching to anyone else if they were guaranteed one day to be taken from me? It caused terrible pain.

    The progressive and relevant point here is that her memory lives and there are so many lessons attached to her memory. Mommy says that she and a family friend ministered to Aunt Val within the context of Christianity – the whole concept of ensuring that one's soul is right before one transitions into eternity. It was Aunt Val's feeling at the time that she wanted to commit to God, but there were shortcomings she felt she needed to address to make it right.

And so mommy told me that she assured Aunt Val that a relationship with the Most-High cannot be obtained through human effort alone, but by surrendering the soul to His spirit – to conform and allow God to do His work within His creation. This is because God is beyond merciful and we, as a global citizenry, are protected by His grace. Coincidentally at the time, Aunt Val's favorite gospel song was, *"Your Grace and Mercy"* by the Mississippi Mass Choir. She was a believer that *"God's mercy brought her through."* Very often Christians utter, *"His grace is sufficient."* That is quite true.

The human being, whether male, female or hermaphrodite, is composed of the body, soul and spirit. Our animate bodies are reflecting the internal fight between the soul and spirit. There is no wickedness in God so He is only spirit. That is why we are saved by mercy and grace because without it, God and His purity could not remotely associate with us.

Like an umbilical cord, our spirits are attached to God so that we can have a relationship with Him. Because impurity dare not contaminate the Most-High, in order to experience God entirely, we must approach Him in the correct alignment. The soul must be conformed to our spirit and our spirits conformed to Jehovah. So it follows that the mind is linked to our soul and spirit, yet the spirit can only think about pure things – those things which are not even conceivable to the soul.

The spirit thinks about those ideas which link to God. The soul dreams and ponders things linked to the

Earth and human desires. When the Creator communicates to our spirit, His messages force the soul to conform in such a way that can "wow" extending to the empowerment of other human beings.

For example, in the art of acrobats, a gymnast is trained to balance and focus. The celebrity gymnast on a winning occasion might have simply given the access to the Almighty to supernatural levels of performance. Only God's landing is a perfect 10! If gymnasts rely on solely their souls rather than soul and spirit, just perhaps those gymnasts will break their necks! Human estimation by the most advanced soul could not be fully correct, just as Katherine Johnson of NASA, could not exactly provide the correct coordinates for the first American landing on the moon.

While science in any form provides very concrete facts, it remains concrete or "compelling" as an adjective but could never produce the original material to create concrete itself. That is left for the Creator of the universe. Only He can create a person, place or thing – period! Science could only clone, create, improve or attempt to explain what is already there.

The universe is drawn to unfold because of its Creator's grace – and His grace alone. It cannot be rebutted that the sciences have brought advancement to the human race and our environments. However, the same can be said for the destruction it has brought as well. The latter can be seen as a crime against God's creation, yet He allows the

Earth to continue its orbit. This proves He is merciful bearing a forgiveness that surpasses human understanding.

Jehovah's benevolence supplies an ever-powerful blueprint as to the gift of forgiveness. Since some of us are so boldly criminal against the very creation of the Most-High, should we dare ask, *"Why does He allow us to die in natural disasters when we contribute to them"*? I should like to believe the Eternal Father is perfect, but just perhaps He allows the bad to happen some of the time since we seem not to get the lesson most of the time.

And just perhaps this claim can touch the hearts of men in terms of daily interaction with others to choose good over evil. Just perhaps this message can discourage the very thought of hurting others because you can temporarily get away with it for a cheap thrill or laugh or feel of temporary power, but this evil will not be maintained.

Because God grants life, we as human beings should strive to do right by others, forgive them when it is required, as we learn also to forgive ourselves. How do we expect God to forgive us when we have become so hell-bent on not forgiving others? Indeed, God does not carry a heart of man.

I can recall a very inspiring piece I wrote for an internal competition at my job as a Customer Service Representative called, "I Tell Truth" which declares that:

> I tell truth,
> And the truth that I tell,
> Roars louder than any human clout;

You see integrity is a value,
Of individuals who stand out;

For when one lacks integrity,
It weakens success;
Failure will arise,
Because it goes against everything,
Meant to bless;

We, the human race,
Should love our sister, our brother,
And not destroy each other,
Doing unto others,
What is expected for ourselves;

Such ancient advice,
Passed down through generations,
To the very foundation of nations;
It is a mighty power!

And as the family unit,
Is meant to stay together,
Pray and play together,
It reveals the promise,
That as a people, united,
We are one despite diversity;

Let us understand one another,
From our hearts and souls;
It will uplift us all;
You and me,
And those we cannot see,
Our quality of living; through love,

The way we interact,
Is meant to impact;
Whether amidst new faces,
Or behind the scenes,
From open or tight spaces;

It attracts positively,
By those who feel embraced;
Strengthening relationships,
The proof that respect is in place;

The universe deserves our best.
Need I tell lies? Need you?
Need I explain that we, humans, are the world too?
That's why I advocate for the cause,
Standing tall,
On principle,
And that is unity for us all –
I tell truth.

At the time that the poem was written and submitted to the competition, my country endured Hurricane Dorian during which very many people succumbed to drowning. Destiny is ringing in my ears that it was not intended to be written for that competition, but to be expressed exactly as it is being expressed at this moment. The reason why is that it speaks to the standard of mercy we should aspire to obtain while we live on Earth.

The Creator has made us to learn lessons as we navigate throughout life's amazing journey. We are not expected to be Him, but we are encouraged to live similar to Him. By this I mean our spirit should line up. If God is merciful, which He undoubtedly is, we should look to His standard of mercy. His mercy is without condition and endless. He forgives in depths that are incomparable to the depth of a human being. The story of Jesus Christ provides a wonderful example.

The Bible teaches that Christ Jesus, God incarnate, knew the offences of proud and snobby people. How could we attempt to deny knowledge of the modern-day Sadducee and Scribe? They form the unduly proud and stiff-upper-lip of societies worldwide who belittle others. They puff up social class, academia and self-accomplishment.

And how could we deny the humiliation of Christ Jesus extending even to the poor but rich at heart? These are the people who openly squawk and scorn others with spit, jokes and two-faced backstabbing. Yet, as Christ was judged and stomped upon, He humbly begged His very own merciless nature, His Father in Zion to, *"forgive them, for they know not what they do?"*

I invite you to a time in your life or, even hypothetically speaking, when you were put in a predicament where your integrity was questioned; you were thrown against the wall where you were being attacked by a person or persons you knew you could destroy. How did you feel? Did you fight back or did you allow the situation to settle peacefully?

Bear in mind, you possess the power to destroy – not necessarily to kill, but to destroy and permanently prove the point that you could. How did it feel in either of those scenarios whether you reacted positively or negatively? And worse, the people that are offending you are people you helped. Imagine that.

This is the balance of mercy – to be merciful or merciless. Remember, you are a king or queen. What do you do? How much are you expected to take? How does one react in a position of power when the best advice is that when one is put in a position of power one must learn to be merciful?

My good friend, Dave, taught me a very crucial lesson on being merciful. A mutual friend and I were going through a very rough patch and we were not seeing eye-to-eye for weeks. Dave found himself in the middle of it because the three of us spoke regularly on the phone three-way. Somehow, our mutual friend started to speak a bit too often about me when I was not around. It was not in a bad way, but Dave began feeling that we were adults who needed merely to address the dispute and resolve the matter.

Eventually Dave brought us together as an unbiased mediator because he knew how bull-headed we could be. Although I agreed to this seemingly kind approach, I addressed the disagreement rather viciously. I was unable to stop. Dave allowed me to vent and afterwards interjected that he saw my challenge. He was able to recognize what had been a flaw for many years. His words were, *"Angelo, you have got to learn to exercise mercy."*

My appreciation for Dave magnified that day because he, without the fear of backlash, identified my underlying issue and was honest enough to expose it. This is not to say that I was completely to blame, but mercy is an essential ingredient to the art of forgiveness.

You see God in His infinite power can do anything He wants to anybody, anything or anywhere for a taste of doom; yet, He infrequently does. The nature of human beings, for the most part is carnal, so there is sometimes hunger to be self-destructive.

God, on the other hand, grants us many chances because He knows the way we live, love and learn. With this knowledge God is just and treats us accordingly. He forgives us often and will punish us when necessary.

The true meaning of mercy is the ability to accept that we are all capable of making mistakes. When others offend us, rather than automatically becoming angry, we ought to appreciate that our interpretation of their actions might not have been the desired intention.

Unless the infraction against you is outright, consider retraction of revenge and mercilessness. We might fail once or twice – it is never easy, but worth a try. Besides, we as the human race, regularly offend the Creator so if we expect forgiveness from Him, we must forgive consistently.

CHAPTER FIFTEEN
Our God Avenges

"Dearly beloved, avenge not yourselves, but rather give place unto wrath: for it is written, Vengeance is mine; I will repay, saith the Lord."
Romans 12:19

For many this chapter will be a very uncomfortable read. This is because in our minds, it is most desirable to believe that a father-figure is there solely to comfort and protect us. The human mind only grasps that which is human. But it must be realized that God is not human; He is spirit, and his decisions as King of kings sometimes require that He allows the unthinkable to happen in order to protect us from ourselves. This includes "breaking" us. Human beings are very selfish by nature. We are born alone to die alone no matter how we attempt to trick ourselves that we can be entirely selfless.

Think about it. When there is an announcement made with respect to loss of cabin pressure pre-take-off aboard any flight, we are advised to place the air mask on ourselves before we attempt to assist fellow passengers. I highly doubt that a decision to assist fellow passengers before ourselves would happen if we know we would die. This is because we are created to survive. It is indeed a battle of the fittest. A spirit being, which is immortal, thinks differently.

From a Christian perspective, we believe that Christ Jesus was the ultimate sacrifice. As God can foretell every event under the sun, He became flesh to experience what we feel knowing that He would be crucified by His own creation. The point is our Creator is entirely selfless; we are not. This is proved by questioning oneself, "If I knew that Jack will kill me, will I let him, or will I defend myself"? Unless you are suicidal, you will defend yourself and that is not negotiable, correct?

Now a mother, even more likely than a father, might consider otherwise when faced with a decision between life and death. In fact, how many of you mothers would risk your lives say you and any number of your offspring were attacked by a grizzly bear? Bear in mind, in this possible instance, that you are holding onto your baby boy and you unfortunately dropped him trying to get away. How many of you, upon seeing that the grizzly is about to harm your baby boy, will run back to protect him knowing that your chance of survival is very slim? It makes you think does it not? Yet, I know beyond a reasonable doubt that if God is faced with the same predicament, He will run to His child without a flinch and defend to the extent of murder.

Let us remember that the Most-High is the Am that I Am, and as a Creator, He will have had a vision of His creation. We are said to be created in His image and likeness. If we are capable of becoming angry to the extent of murder, can't God kill? We can only think of things installed by the Creator. We call it evil, but evil was birthed of evil that was, too, created by the Almighty. Be clear, though,

God is not evil. All things whether good or bad will have been conceived by our Everlasting Father. Many stories throughout the passage of time prove that God's wrath can be severe. He builds and He destroys!

For example, according to Exodus 32:14, *"And the Lord repented of the evil which he thought to do unto his people."* Interesting isn't it? I assert God is most merciful, but God too can be merciless. The Bible also recounts the story of how angels came down and procreated with women. They were the days of the *"nephilims"* or giants that roamed the Earth. They died out during the age of Noah and the flood. God flooded the Earth without regret and they drowned.

How about Sodom and Gomorrah that is referenced by Christians to dehumanize the LGBTQ community? Subject to the laws mandated in Leviticus, the city was destroyed for all manner of sexual perversion inclusive of heterosexual abominations! God sent warning, but relentlessly rendered His verdict. If God created the creators of Isis and the Taliban, for example, and they too were created in the image and likeness of God, then it is universally acceptable to suggest that even hell and the epitome of terrorism here on Earth know no terror like the Living God.

Our daddy in Zion created typhoons and earthquakes! His terror can be heard in the cracking thunder, howling winds and torrential rainfall! His presence can be felt like the clash of avalanches and the infliction of the deadliest of plagues! There is no fury that can compare to the fury of God! Deep down, we all know better. We know He is not the one with whom to play! *He Avenges Children.*

Personal experience has been my best teacher. In fact, I refer to one Scottish-born teacher from my past that I have forgiven but shan't forget. She taught me the influence of prejudice and supports the adage that children are impressionable. Being my Math teacher, I initially enjoyed her class. I gained interest because I liked the way she taught. As time progressed, I developed the trust to ask questions and to approach her when I did not understand something. Whatever attitudes were underlying her impression of me was well disguised because I felt comfortable enough with her being my Math teacher.

But one day that all changed. I was seeking clarity on Algebra and was sent to the Principal's office because apparently, I was *"rude"* and *"gesticulated too much."* What must be borne in mind is that I was maintaining an "A" average in her class. As a child, I knew that in order to keep my grades up, I had better ask questions when I did not understand something. I agree I could have been a wee-bit of a spoilt brat, but rude?

When I arrived at the Principal's office, somehow even the Principal who knew better was convinced against her better judgment, deciding to call mommy to school. One thing I was raised knowing is if mommy was called to school, it had better be a damn good reason. Mommy was one who *"worked hard for her money"* and she maintained that if she was called from her job, the only way to escape a *"cut ass"* (whooping) is either achievement or a defense.

Mommy was adamant that all I was sent to school to do was learn and become smarter. I could already tell I did nothing wrong because I simply asked the Math teacher questions that she was paid to answer. Whether or not I was overly persistent was not my issue, it was my then teacher's issue; one which simply required that she managed her class effectively considering that every student learns differently.

Mommy is known to be a big, curvy and beautiful woman. She wore stilettos that day and every impact of her thick heels made my heart pound a bit harder. I cringed. Her look alone screamed I had got some tall explaining to do for the Principal to invite her to the office.

It was stated that I was rude and was being too disruptive. My mother, as I can recall, gave my math teacher sufficient time to clarify if she found me rude or merely **"talkative"** or "persistent." But instead, she took that risky route of maintaining her view that I was a rude child. Mommy wanted to ensure before she unleashed my hellish "whoop ass" that the claim was unanimous. When mommy wanted something she got it. She demanded that all teachers be invited to the office for questioning and she did not give a *"rat's tit"* if they were teaching mid-lesson.

To mommy's mind was if she could be called off her job, so could all my teachers. Every teacher who came admitted I was quite talkative, but all disagreed that I was a rude child. Mommy grew vicious. I could see it in her eyes, and if she rocked back and forth with clasped hands in her lap, she could kill.

After the last teacher left, mommy requested she had a word with the teacher and principal while I was not in the room. I knew it was war. I left as instructed and sat out front at the reception. As I sat I felt assured somewhat that I was not in trouble because I spoke the truth. No matter how that Math teacher lied that I had done something untoward, her attempt to do so backfired fair and square.

When my opponent reemerged, I learned that a white woman's face could become tomato-ripe-red. At that time I did not know, but I came to understand years later what was discussed. I asked mommy and let us just say just perhaps that math teacher learned a lesson in race relations.

The predominance of blacks in The Bahamas does not accept prejudice. Sometimes we pretend well, as Bahamians, that it does not exist, but it is very real in the country. Proof is in the pudding. Bahamian politics is rooted in racism and class prejudice. There are scattered communities in which such an asinine attitude roams. Having come to The Bahamas from Scotland, when my alma mater became *"too black"* she and like-minded counterparts flocked to where it became "too white."

It was quite alarming when a white, former schoolmate told me to my face post-graduation that our beloved school went down when the Baptist took over from the Lutheran and more Blacks go there. Her stupidity was brought to her attention because I identify as Black so exactly what was she saying to me and so comfortably? Or need I say disrespectfully? How confidently dumb!

No race is exempt from the reality of racism. If you are remotely prejudiced against any race being a racist, you are beyond ignorant; you are very dumb and stupid – point blank! I shall not retract from this truth either because we live in quite an evolving world where tolerance at minimum is the way forward. *He avenges adults.*

My work career has outlined some very interesting scenarios. I was once a child, but there comes a point when we grow up to the bigger picture. At one point I was employed as an English and Commerce teacher at a local high school. It went very well during my tenure because it was an opportunity to learn about personalities and how best to manage them. The most demonic adult cannot compare to a wild teen experiencing puberty.

What began to happen was, despite my hard work, I was not being paid my salary. At first I was patient and accepted the excuses for non-payment on the faith that I would somehow be paid eventually. That Principal, may he rest in eternal peace, extended excuses after excuses and apparently this appeal was not personal. Many teachers working at the institution were experiencing the same hardship and some even attempted a legal recourse to no winning resolution. No case against the Principal was successful.

My knowledge of contract law led me to make the decision to draft a contract because verbal agreement is not as strong. Unless it can be proved through some type of paper trail or witness that there was some line of agreement, it presents the challenge of word against word. However, when a written agreement outlines specifically what is obligated by one or two parties and signatures are signed, there is no way to really dispute a claim unless there is forgery. The Principal's signature was the mistake that set precedence for the school.

My not attending Bar School delayed the process because when I applied to the court, I brought an action against the Principal and not the institution. After finding out the process, further evidence was uncovered which I actually did not want to expose; yet natural justice forced that it would be brought to the light.

Almost losing my case, I was forced to present evidence that pressed my former boss. Either he paid my outstanding salary by the set date or face jail time for the school's accumulated debt. His failure to pay me by the court-ordered date landed him in prison anyway. It must be remembered that I was very patient and understanding leading up to the judgment that began brimming over. Justice was served – wages paid in full.

One last experience where God vindicated me as an adult was at the age of thirty-one. I became an Operations Manager for a short period at a Tourism Concierge Agency. I worked under a very lovely team of Managers except for one. That Manager in particular happened to be the owner's sister who mistreated staff in very sneaky and patronizing ways.

One such incident which transpired landed me one-on-one in a chair where I sit across from what I would call a "bully in heels" flaunting secret powers. There was no one other than me, her and the Creator in that office. It was my word against hers. I can remember as I recount this incident the feeling I felt; one of absolute powerlessness. I felt so low and mistreated for whatever reason. My humble outcry was *"God is my vindicator."* If the devil could cross his legs while he gloats, it was her incarnate. I was left in tears because the situation was so unfair. I regained my dignity and left like nothing ever happened, offering up a prayer with the assurance that God would handle it.

Some months passed and eventually I got another opportunity to work elsewhere. It entailed moving back into an area that I was already used to but I had gained more skill and knowledge. What I found rather interesting looking back at it, is that even when I left the company, there was still an inner desire for justice to prevail because not only was I affected, but so many persons were hurt by the likes of this Manager. I never really had anything nice to say about her so I tried my best not to speak about her at all other than the injustice she caused.

One day I was exiting my vehicle to go into the grocery store and a former coworker approached me. It was a jolly reunion. After all the hugs and laughs the topic had been steered to the Manager from hell. Apparently, she had been fired by her brother and sent home to Jamaica. I was told she had been stealing, but I would not put that on the record because it is hearsay. Even if that were not the reason, the news was brought to my attention even when I was not looking for it. It indicated that former colleagues were equally waiting for the day she would be removed so as not to be oppressed.

Redemption is sweet because our Creator avenges. He sees everything and He knows everything. The sure thing that makes life easier is the fact that in the eyes of the Almighty, no human is above another, for we are all equal under one God. We are all children of the universe and wondrously made. God avenges the well-spoken, the oppressed and the incapable.

Think about it. If we are all children of a very important king here on Earth, are we not considered royal? It is no different when it comes to our Heavenly Father. So if it is the case that we are all His children, that means He does not love one prince or princess more than the other.

Because we all are guilty of sin, we really need not preoccupy ourselves with the judgment of others. The Most-High sits on the throne of Justice as He looks high, just as He looks low. And so another Face of God bears the eyes of Justice. Yahweh is the Lord of law lords with a mega-insight and thus, a rationale that will continue to puzzle mankind.

CHAPTER SIXTEEN
Jehovah - The Just

You might meet me and find out that I am not a fan of tattoos. I like how they look on other people, but I do not get excited about them covering my body-made-in-heaven. I am laughing so loudly right now. Could it be that I am jealous? Besides, when the body is chiseled, just perhaps tattoos would be a good idea, but not when your body resembles a flat tire!

More seriously it does not come before me to judge people who adorn themselves with tattoos — that is up to them — in fact, cover their entire body if they will. I believe our bodies should return to the Creator closest to the way they came to this planet with understandable scars here and there. That is how I feel. Now if I ever were forced to wear a tattoo to save my life, I would proudly consider tattooing the words, *"Only God Can Judge Me."* My soul stirs up when I say those words because they are pure, unadulterated truth.

My Christian upbringing taught me that in order to better understand spiritual things, I can use natural things to compare, contrast and analyze. So to arrive at my point, I shall go back to the days when I attended law school. A topic I found most fascinating is the Rule of Law which asserts that, *"no man is above the law"* to the degree that every man is subject to the law. Moreover, what were also captivating were the concepts of Natural Justice, which is, the Law of the Divine, Morality and Conscience as compared to Man's Law – the Law of Statute, Judicial Precedence and Equity.

We must understand that Jehovah is the Ultimate Judge and the Lord of Hosts. His Court of Law exists in the heavenly realm and so His officers are the angels and spirit beings which encamp about His Majesty. Just as bailiffs, policemen and lawyers keep "a check" on mankind in the natural realm, Jehovah judges from the Throne of Justice using His hosts in Heaven or whomever He chooses to deliver our fate here on Earth. As we are well aware, God is our Ruler. He has created the Ten Commandments which form the basis of law and morality. His grace extends mercy evolving from the harsh laws of the Old into the hopeful laws of the New Testament. It would appear that love is the greatest gift and defense to humanity. It is declared in the Good Book that love is the Greatest Commandment.

Man's law is structured. Having studied law within the English Legal system, a very simplified explanation is that there are statutes (strict, black-letter law), judicial precedents (case law or past rulings of Judges) and equity (principles of conscience and fairness). The way the Courts of law operate is when the lawyer argues statute *or "stated law in books"* and the law is simply too strict or provides no helpful advice due to the facts of the case, case law is then referenced. Indeed statutes outline what is legal and what is not as well as the punishment for breaking the law. Past decisions by Judges provide remedies which soften the ruling to encourage fairer outcomes. The Law of Equity guides the verdict in the name of conscience which seeks to achieve the highest level of justice.

Our Creator sits on the Throne of Grace as He looks high and low. We can hide our evil from mankind, but not from Jehovah! That is because He is omniscient possessing a thorough knowledge of His creation and our thoughts pertaining to everything in it. An example that I can use that proves that Agape love and divine justice surpass all forms of human love is a typical criminal case in which the victim is allegedly murdered.

As humans, it is almost automatic to attack the accused with the words, *"Hang em' high."* This attitude suggests that the accused is automatically guilty until proven innocent. But how is this fair? Should accused people be automatically treated this way when they might not even be linked to the crime? Even more, how could this be if the matter has not been heard in Court? Further, does not the verdict remain with the judge and jury?

On a more religious front, who appointed mankind to be judge and jury of sin when we are all guilty of sin? We are all awaiting trial in the same court of sin, and no sin is greater than the other. No judge is more equipped to interpret and apply the law like Jehovah, so there should be no attempt to do His Job with the remote belief that one can do it better. Not only is God the strongest symbol of Agape love, Jehovah is the law! That is why a man is presumed innocent until proven guilty.

If the Creator judged humans the way we judge each other, I believe humanity would not exist. In fact before I studied law, I was guilty of that quick-judgment because my emotions took over. Emotions, however, do not allow a fairer and thorough consideration of facts. The thing is I was taught that within Criminal Law not only is the **"action"** to be proved, but it must be proved that the accused **"intended"** to kill beyond a reasonable doubt.

The definition of murder and kill are different. Someone is murdered when the killer had maliciously intended to do so whereas a person can be labeled a killer even when he had no intention to kill. So long as a person is killed, any person linked to the death is the killer, but not necessarily a murderer. The definition of kill or murder rests on the distinction between intention and no intention to do so. In British law *"malicious aforethought"* or *"guilty mindset"* or *"premeditation"* determines murder. On the other hand the killing of a person that has been established, but without intention, is manslaughter since a person has died.

"How does this all tie in", you might ask. Well, there are conflicts brewing worldwide as to who pleases God in theory and practice of religion to extremes of murder. One of my favorite legal principles when I studied law is, *"he who comes to equity, must come with clean hands."* In terms of judging others and religious discussion, what this means simply is you should not bash others expecting to be rewarded in a good way. Your bashing will not go unpunished – point blank!

Thus, it follows that many people across religions take a rather judgmental approach when it comes to who they are in relation to the Most-High. When we become arrogant and believe that personal conviction is the truth against everything else is not admirable to God. Again, who has appointed mankind to that seat of judgment?

To make this point clearer, consider that we both are royalty. We are both children of a very powerful king. Your name is Mystery and my name is Mysterious. One of the rules in the palace is that there is to be no use of swear words and there is to be no stealing cookies from the cookie jar. Now say I went to our father, the king, and said, father, *"Mystery is such an ass! You told us not to steal the cookies and now the cookie jar is broken!"*

Before I ask the begging question, swearing in this context is like judging others just as stealing cookies is to believing in another religion. Who do you believe the King will chastise? Is it fair to punish me, you or both of us? I should like to think the both of us, correct? If we are all sinners, how do we judge each other by esteeming one sin or perspective above another?

Within Christianity, one of the biggest examples of this is the hostility against gays on the foundation of Sodom and Gomorrah. I guess only gays lived there? That is highly unlikely. I guess the actions of Lot and his daughters were not incestuous? But the story mentions that his daughters attempted to bed their father, so Lot was transgender I suppose? How am I so confused even though the book of Leviticus spells it out? Is it not written that all manner of sexual perversion is an abomination to God including those committed by heterosexuals? It is so typical for the Bible to be taken out of context and used for some "church agenda."

Sexual perversions include the adulterer, the fornicator, incestuous relations and the enjoyment of bestiality so spare me the nonsense please.

Appropriately, the words of the Bible, or any scripture for that matter are subject to interpretation. Faith in the Preacher, Rabbi, or the Guru is wise, but spiritual revelation to self indeed is the masterful way forward. For example, having attended law school coupled with the fact that I have begun to enjoy writing, I share the Doctrine of Statutory Interpretation that applies three general rules with respect to written law and thus can be applied to general interpretations of words:

Literal: *Understanding the written law word for word.*
Golden: *Understanding written law is intended to avoid an absurd or ineffective result.*
Mischief: *Understanding what wrongs are written law intended to deter and correct.*

I remember when I was an English Instructor at a technical and vocational institute and had to teach the four levels of understanding. Interestingly, they are:

<u>Literal:</u>	Understanding words as they are expressed.
For example:	Donna is a lady of the night.
Literal Interpretation:	Donna prefers the night.
<u>Figurative:</u>	Understanding words for their hidden or symbolic meaning.

For example:	Donna is a lady of the night.
Figurative Interpretation:	Donna is a prostitute.
<u>Applied</u>:	Understanding words to form a founded conclusion.
For example:	Donna is a lady of the night.
Applied Interpretation:	Donna, being a lady of the night, suggests that she either prefers to be out at night or she is a prostitute.
<u>Judgmental</u>:	Understanding words to form an opinion or argument.
For example:	Donna is a lady of the night.
Judgmental interpretation:	Donna, being a lady of the night, is immoral regardless of her preference.

While this information is impressive, it still does not provide guidance as to the interpretation regarding laws of the spirit. The natural and the supernatural are two separate and distinct realms. The way we relate to the natural realm is through soul and flesh. Our deepest intellect can be attained at that level, but no intellect can compare to the intellect of the supernatural lest it be revealed.

Interestingly enough, the Law of Man has been created, founded and guided by the conscience of mankind, yet the most divine reference is the Law of Moses that was outlined on the scrolls. Those laws are very much the foundation of many legal systems. Debatably, none of us existed at that time to either approve or disprove that those laws were actually mandated by the Creator. Those who remotely entertain the possibility rely on faith.

What becomes factual is personal experience and not necessarily coincidence. Spiritual interpretation requires either revelation through either meditation or introspection. In other words, "hindsight is always 20/20." From a Christian perspective consider the following: Psalm 121:7 states, *"The Lord shall preserve thee from all evil: he shall preserve thy soul."*

Christianity maintains in simpler terms, *"Who God keeps is well kept."* Moreover, 2 Chronicles 16:22 declares, *"Touch not mine anointed, and do my prophets no harm."*

It is my position that the two scriptures referenced are examples of divine law and refer to those who operate in the Spirit of the Living God.

I remember a time that proves how the Lord renders a verdict. I was working at an establishment that involved a lot of detailed documentation. I managed to do well most of the time, but sometimes I would mess up here and there – to err is human, is it not?

But on this particular occasion, coupled with a series of unfair scenarios I faced, a certain error arose that was brought to my attention. Upon review of the reported error, I found that I was correctly guided and thus, followed the correct procedure. It should be restated that there were a number of issues that I faced that were unjust and was brought to the attention of those in charge. It will have seemed from where I sat to be a conspiracy of some kind to force me to quit or get me terminated.

Months before I had been offered a position as a Supervisor, and after prayer and a response from the Creator, I chose not to accept the offer on the feeling that, "I wished to earn the position and that titles do not impress me." I am happy that I did not join that team because that very trio of Supervisors proved to be either unconsciously or consciously unjust to not only me but my fellow colleagues.

There came a time when I initiated Human Resources with my grievance that the treatment of staff by the trio in question was not the way forward. Apologies were given as well as indifference. I distinctly remember the warning, however, that I know like I know the Most-High mouthed in the atmosphere, *"When you are put in the position of power, learn to be merciful."*

Months later, the company closed, as well as the termination of the referenced trio made known. Yet, I still retained my job. Proving a very important point, the Bible advises that, "Obedience is better than sacrifice." I was obedient in that I did not accept the position based on the answer to my prayer sacrificing the possibility of a raise. Looking back the verdict was not coincidence, but evidence of my faith. God rendered a verdict based upon scripture in line with my position that the divine is just. Jehovah's words will continually be proven, thus, to my mind, they present truth to support my individual faith - my personal relationship with the Almighty.

It is not my job to argue that God is real, discrediting other personal revelations; my lifestyle is simply to share this good news and live happily convinced of God's goodness – simple.

We know Jehovah judges in ways pass finding out. When I think of the story of Noah and the Ark, His final decision to flood the Earth was one of passion. To allow it to rain for so many days and nights suggests that Jehovah must have wholeheartedly desired that there would be no life on the face of the Earth except for those aboard the Ark. Yet we have seen many times throughout the story of life where God has extended redemption, bliss and mercy.

As a Christian I rely on the words of the Bible in Psalms 7:11 that, *"God is a just judge, and God is angry with the wicked every day."* It is encouraged that we all do right by each other so that our deeds may be favorable in the eyes of our Universal Creator.

CHAPTER SEVENTEEN
The Color of God

I was raised as an Anglican having grown accustomed to the clear, sometimes rainbow-bright stained glass version of biblical characters around the cathedrals of worship. The services were so *"Church of England"* and I do not mean this in an offensive way at all. It is just a personalized expression of exactly how formal Anglo-sermons tend to be. It was not until I would become an exchange student to Sweden did I learn that stained glass could reveal such a uniquely different outlook on a possibly forbidden truth. It was the start of unlearning everything that I thought was the truth: unlearning the proverbial way and the light. The revelation did not dawn on me until most recently and it shows that when Our Creator reveals a thing, it is well revealed and understood.

Attending high school in Sweden was an unforgettable experience. What I appreciate even now as a former foreign exchange student is the expectation that I will have taken the opportunity, not only to experience another culture of the destination to which I was assigned, but also to travel outside that country. And so such day came that I was presented with an option that exposed me to deeper truth.

Apart from Swedish for Immigrants also called "Special Swedish", I studied Italian, Spanish, Math, English, Swedish Language and Drama under the Humanities Program. It was a delightful combination. But the subject which bridged the shocking insight was Spanish studies.

Students were invited to sign up for a mini two-week exchange program during which the applicant could stay with a family and be engaged by Spanish culture. I called back home to The Bahamas and mommy and daddy agreed to sponsor the adventure.

I have no regrets. The visit was mesmerizing! From my wonderful host family, to the enchanting locals of Loja, Granada, to the delicious food and flamenco dance and festivities, I was enthralled by everything Spanish. There were a number of excursions planned for the group of us who travelled to Malaga, Spain from Stockholm, the capital of Sweden. We were split into two groups. One group was assigned to families in Loja, Granada of which I was a part, and the other group was assigned to families in Huétor, Granada.

The excursion that actually pricked me, spiritually, was a tour of a church not so far from Loja that was gorgeous inside. Most intriguing was the stained glass that depicted black people. It was rather strange to me. So being a curious teenager, I could not help but to ask the Tour Guide uncomfortable questions when she invited them.

Imagine being the only black student on this tour – literally. Every other student was white. Imagine having been taught, raised, and influenced to accept that the portrait of "White Jesus" is the Son of Man. Imagine that – t'was having everything I know challenged in that moment. And even if I wanted to challenge it, the actors in the movies that I grew up watching around the Easter and Christmas were everything but black. Can we disprove that fact? Who wants to acknowledge that Jesus Christ was not white? In fact how many blacks in Euro-influenced societies and books are so bold as to give credit where it is due? But I digress.

So I asked the Tour Guide if she could be so kind as to explain why there were stained glass images of black people. I was at least open enough to grasp that the depictions were telling some of the well-known stories in the Bible. The Tour Guide confirmed her doubt that I was indeed not from Sweden, but was invited upon return there or The Bahamas to research the Bible. Her reason was, *"you would come to find that many characters in The Bible are your complexion."*

I was beyond dumbfounded by her answer as the quietness awoke the awkward silence of crickets surround-sound. Even though light was shed on a very controversial topic in favor of my race, it was buried for the remainder of my exchange program.

Years later, after I returned to The Bahamas, I was working as a Front Desk Clerk at a boutique hotel. At that time a bellman invited me to his church where teachings not so much in favor of a *"White Jesus"* were introduced to my life. Too, very compelling evidence was used to verify the claim. The question that formed the basis of many presentations at the non-denominational church was, *"Which Jesus"*? I was there for a season, but there is no need to go into detail of what was said other than to share a briefing of what was learned. It must be included that just perhaps this was being taught at other churches in The

Bahamas, but possibly I did not get the memo until the right season in my life.

Nevertheless, very recently, I was surfing the worldwide web and was very drawn to passionate debates about Jesus' race between the descendants of the Jews of Israel and a sect who identify themselves as "Black Hebrew Israelites." The Israeli descended Jew's argument was on the biblical scripture:

> *"... Now he was ruddy, and withal of a beautiful countenance, and goodly to look to."*
> 1 Samuel 16:12

Secondly, another scripture was referenced:

> *"My beloved is white and ruddy, the chiefest among ten thousand."*
> Song of Solomon 5:10

The Hebrew Israelites argued:

> *"His head and his hairs were white like wool, as white as snow; and his eyes were as a flame of fire; and his feet like unto fine brass, as if they burned in a furnace; and his voice as the sound of many waters."*
> Revelations 1:14-15

In turn, the Jews were likening the word "ruddy" as a "rich" expression of pigment on a white person. I do not believe that this is at all in line with what "ruddy" means in this context. Are proponents suggesting that Jesus Christ had a sad case of Rosacea?

Being "white" in this context could have symbolized the purity of Jesus. It is suggested that when white people are richly red, the redness is rarely all over the body, but in part. Redness on white people indicates blushing, embarrassment and their feeling flushed or exhausted. I have grown up around white people and there are interracial marriages in my family so it is obvious to see. If I did not have enough experience with family, what beats an entire year of my life abroad in a predominantly white country like Sweden?

The Hebrew Israelites present a more lucid position, in my view, but understandably the Israeli Jews would not entertain them, not only because the Hebrew Israelites promote a borderline militia-like agenda, but they can appear borderline-racist in their approach.

Certainly, African Americans, who seem to make up a large fraction of the movement, were likely fuelled, in part, by the intensity of racism in the United States of America. I am not a Hebrew Israelite, but I see a vision of a darker hue when I think of their reference to Revelations 1:14-15. This allows me to look into the mirror with a stronger sense of pride when I think of the scripture, *"So God created man in his own image, in the image of God created he him; male and female created he them."* Genesis 1:27

Further, there is a persuasive listing by the Hebrew Israelites of the 12 Tribes of Judah in accordance with Isaiah 11:11 that states: *"And it shall come to pass in that day, that the Lord shall set his hand again the second time to recover the remnant of his people, which shall be left, from Assyria, and from Egypt, and from Pathros, and from Cush, and from Elam, and from Shinar, and from Hamath, and from the islands of the sea."*

Thus, it was claimed by the Black Hebrew Israelites that the tribes of Israel are:

- Judah – Negroes
- Benjamin – West Indians
- Levi – Haitians
- Ephraim – Puerto Rico
- Mannasseh – Cubans
- Simeon – Dominicans
- Reuben – Seminole Indians
- Gad – American Indians
- Naphtali – Argentina and Chile
- Zebulon – Guatemala to Uruguay
- Asher – Colombia to Uruguay
- Issachar – Mexican Indians

One only needs to look at the human race and it is clear that blacks naturally have wooly hair, as well as a myriad of different textures of hair. Jesus' hair could have simply turned gray or white early in His life just as some young black men like myself go salt and pepper.

His eyes resembling the flames of fire could be anywhere between hazel and light brown because that eye color is so typical among fair to medium-brown blacks. Think Rihanna or Michael Ealy or Tyra Banks or Terrance Howard. Coupled with their skin resembling burnt, fine brass and their eyes being like the flames of fire, it would appear that Jesus was colored somehow.

Even if Jesus was not black, He indeed was not white. The word ruddy, I humbly submit, simply portrays the undertone of Christ. His race, whatever we can conceive it to be, must resemble races of undertones that are red. The citizenry of Jerusalem strike me as a lighter hue nowadays, but there is no telling the racial composition back then because none of us were actually there.

Curiosity throughout the years of my life encouraged me to read a few books here and there. Some useful information that I can share at this juncture are concepts of Buddhism, Hinduism and Christianity to illuminate what is most essential when it comes to appreciating the color of God.

Hindus, who follow the religion of Hinduism, believe in one God called "Brahma" who is formless and who can become a form, "Paramatma." Thus, Hindus believe that there are three major qualities of the Almighty God; "Brahma" (formless), "Vishnu" (Creator) and "Shiva" (destroyer). Their sacred book is called the Vedas which is a collection of scriptures Hindus refer to as the "Eternal Knowledge of God." The Vedas or "Shruti" meaning "that which is heard" was formed much like the sacred Torah (Judaism) and Three Baskets of Knowledge (Buddhism).

I remember reading somewhere that the Three Baskets of Knowledge of Buddhism was created 500 years after Buddha. Buddha is not God, nor do Buddhists claim he was. Buddhists pay respect instead to a man who has taught that every human can attain the state of Nirvana, which is a state of enlightenment and inner peace.

Christianity is actually a more recent religious path that was founded out of the testaments that were written, four of which are the gospel: the books of Matthew, Mark, Luke and John.

Now on the simple merit that Hinduism is one of the oldest religions, followed by Buddhism and then Christianity, my previous position several chapters back is reintroduced. The people long before Christianity was founded are not burning in the endless lake of fire. In fact a little research points to spirituality which is connected to Hindus.

The nature of God is eternal so there should be no time stamp placed even on their early scriptures that were heard and passed down through the generations. The same story is told about the Christian Prophets that heard from God and, in turn, wrote down law and accounts that would prove useful to humanity once applied correctly. So religion in its purest sense is a great thing indeed. Abuse of others in the name of religion by human beings is another discussion altogether.

Revelation of the color of God is as mysterious as why we cannot see the Most-High in the first place. How is it that we know He is there, but we cannot see Him? If He created us from the womb of His imagination then One God suggests that He is all inclusive. The long and short of it is He bears a color that is too powerful for us to see with the naked eye. That is because the God of the Universe is a spirit. He bears a color that is unknown. He exists of a complexion that remains unclassified yet identifies and resembles us all.

As a former English teacher, I see that much of the Bible, for instance, is written in metaphor and in ways that should not always be taken literally. There are also scriptures that may seemingly contradict each other, but a string of them used strategically can be very compelling. Our Father in the heavens has blessed us bountifully through His creation.

Comparatively, members of different religions who argue can be seen as a bunch of noisy children in a wealthy king's palace. Some are quiet and well behaved while others are simply too noisy. Quiet, well behaved children reap the rewards. General wrong is argument among supposed princes and princesses of peace over which religion is the correct one. That is loudness. Persons who speak their truth both acknowledging and respecting other points of view in humility tend to reap the blessings from the Almighty. They are the quiet and well-behaved children of the divine.

Arguing that the Messiah has not actually come, Jesus Christ was white, not black and vice versa, or that Prophet Mohammed is the most current Prophet, to state a few examples get us nowhere. Arguments promote so much discord. On the contrary, what we can do is focus on the Spirit of God. This leads us to the spiritual redemption that proves to be much deeper than the color of skin which in all truth fails us. The attitude glorifies flesh insomuch as it is the same spirit that encourages prejudice and racism against humanity. Therefore, it goes against the grain of love and essence of world peace.

God has no skin being a spirit, but can imbue whomever or whatever He chooses to fulfill the evidence that He is real and has always been from the foundation of the universe. There is no fulfilling connection than that of the joining of two or more kindred souls, and equally, no deeper dissatisfaction than when spirits do not mesh well.

Have you ever met someone and think, "I do not take to this person, there is something about this person," yet you have never met the person before? Thus, you wonder how is it that you feel the way you feel? Maybe you have met before because the heart of a man – the soul and spirit is incapable of perceiving time – it is eternal.

I end by sharing a poem I wrote and call,

"Color-less":

When I say I am black,
I must tell you, my spirit blows like the wind.
Then gradually, in a lull, I realize such a feeling erases
History's shame;
Warping my identity, as false as my last name,

Saying I am black,
Makes the truth forbidden,
The undisputed fact, that yesterday,
I was in hiding, born of embarrassment and injustice,
And by today, as time faded,
I cannot claim I am white,

The race of my very own family – who disowned me!
Could I put up a fight since that's not who I am,
categorically?

Even deeper, I am neither black nor white because my
roots incriminate me;
Just as roots stuck in soils of a prison
refusing to let me go,
And so, I am a hybrid of some kind,
Elements of pride and prejudice,
Sometimes playing tricks on my mind
Because when I look at my face,

I see dreamy, squinting eyes – unmatched,
To my very wide nose,
A trait said to defy beauty, among insecure Negroes.
Then I look to my body,
Dipped in caramel, a shade shy of cream and coffee,
More like toffee,
And the question is asked, from deep within,
What color are you?

Am I color-less? A mix?
Since it is safe to say,
Black and white, produces gray;
That gray area;
The confusion, an outright identity illusion,
That begs for closure;
Searching my soul,
I see that I am more than slavery;
A bloodline comprising of West African slaves,
Those caught and shackled and chained,
To be bought, tricked, loaded in ships – like cargo, and

beaten with whips,
I am also a descendant of those spared of mass graves.

Indeed I am akin to ghosts of former concentration camps,
Six feet below weeping for flowers,
The victims of the Holocaust – lost:
To gas chambers and acid showers;

They faced no slave trade or some humiliating buyer's parade,
But the Jews were tortured!
As cruel as sin; headshot, close range!
Bullet riddled, suffocated,
Seemingly not so complicated, for their tainted blood,
Molten skin by acid was the exchange;

Tainted blood? Were they not white?
Oh that's right, they weren't, and they were labeled Jews,
So not only am I neither black nor white,
I am another race refused.

Could I be Latino
Since my great grandfather, just so you know,
He was from Cuba,
He fled, falling in love, having children, cross-bred,
He and my black great grandmother.

Just maybe, my ability to dance,
My loud gesticulation,
The passion you'll see,
Through my quick, bullet-like articulation

Makes me Hispanic,
Because the Spanish live through me;

There is no known record of Mongolia
In my bloodline,
But now I understand the persuasion of Tiger Woods,
Borderline – anger,
His widely being misunderstood
That he could not be black,
But a mix of ebony and Asian
So please refer to him as, "Blasian"!

What color am I?
Extending the powerful question,
"What color are you"?
To encourage the thought,
That we are all somehow mixed;
We are simply – human,
Color-less.

Throughout the hills and valleys of life, the highways and byways will lead us to self-discovery. The saying goes what does not kill you will only make you stronger. True strength is coming to realize we were created with a purpose. Life is so much more than the hue that adorns flesh. Inevitably, flesh will die, plop and rot.

Our power is governed by what is inside of us – the spirit of every human being, collectively. Our salvation is discovering the truth that there can be kindled light within us all, and we should jealously guard against any form of darkness since it takes the light within us to shine bright enough to someday see the lovely Face of God.

CHAPTER EIGHTEEN
God Created with Purpose

The wonderful thing about life and being human is that we have all been created with a purpose, on purpose, for that purpose. Key words in a beautiful poem, "Desiderata" written by Max Ehrmann advises, *"You are a child of the universe, No less than the trees and the stars; You have the right to be here. And whether or not it is clear to you, No doubt the universe is unfolding as it should."*

"[We indeed] have the right to be here"! Like other living things that fill our Biology books, we were designed, altogether, to fulfill a purpose and we should do so without much thought. A team of tiny ants will carry loads multiplying their weight, the chimpanzees will holler to influence other chimpanzees to chime in and mischievously "wild out", and the elephant will playfully spray water from its trunk no matter how monstrous its appearance.

During an engaging conversation recently with a Sudanese friend and fellow Poet, Kamal, we spoke to the simplicity of nature. Using the example of the relationship between a human being and a tree, we discovered a type of mutual respect that was divinely designed. When we breathe we exhale carbon dioxide so the tree can survive. To express its appreciation, we can inhale the oxygen it produces. In a world where we so freely cut trees in exchange for paper, it so freely gives us life – the very oxygen we breathe.

So if plants and animals can coexist in nature with limited intelligence in purpose, what makes it so difficult for us as humans to identify our purpose? Maybe we are reckless with our free will which complicates things when, in fact, the true beauty of life is unlocked by simplicity. However, when we choose to focus on why we are here more seriously, it leads to the very solid truth that we were created with the gift of purpose.

The Most-High made no mistake when He created us. That should provide us with the spark to discover exactly what our purpose is. Affirm it: *"I am made with a purpose, on purpose, for that purpose."*

Taking these claims in turn, let us begin with the phrase, **"with a purpose."** Long before we were born into our current reality, God knew us. He knew us because we were His dream - His vision. And that vision came to pass. He is the Creator of the Universe and everything in it.

As with a natural inventor, any idea is firstly conceived and pondered. Careful consideration measures whether or not what is conceived can in fact become a reality. Once a vision is seen and can be attained, a plan is drafted to accomplish that goal. Every religion tells a version of Our Creator that leads to one truth, that is, He is the Universal Creator. The very word Universe denotes a certain **"oneness"** – **"one verse."** If we are all God's children, then clearly we, as the human race resembling each other, also resemble Him. We form His total offspring and I state this from one of many perspectives; the Christian perspective.

Because Jehovah is the Beginning, and the End, He birthed the beginning and He knows the end. Everything conceived of His being serves a purpose. Yet it must be understood that God is infinite, meaning forever from the past moving forward through eternity. With no actual fixed beginning, He reigns in the present and evermore throughout infinity and beyond.

Having read a little about Hinduism, an engaging Guru channeling his thoughts based on Hindu scriptures would explain that God is a divine consciousness of knowledge without an exact beginning. I can agree drawing a specific reference that all living things are products of that divine consciousness. The story of Creation as outlined in the Bible is merely a version, an addition or edition of what is already evident.

Hinduism being the earliest recorded religion holds strong weight even if not all. This supports the more stable view that all religions hold truth. For example, as a Bahamian, my ancestry is mainly rooted in West Africa. Chiefly sixteen countries form that region. They are Nigeria, Ghana, Ivory Coast, Senegal, Sierra Leone, Niger, Togo, Mali, Liberia, Burkina Faso, Benin, The Gambia, Mauritania, Cape Verde, Guinea and Guinea-Bissau. There is no way of telling exactly if my forefathers of West African descent migrated from other African territories. It is too far back in history. But my genes will confirm that I am a loud voice of the slave. The other side of me is composed of the traces of European lineage that count, but are degraded by the very grim realities of slavery and the Jewish holocaust.

My point is that Bahamian history teaches our students that the first people who resided in The Bahamas were the Arawaks or the Lucayan Indians. The Arawaks were deemed "uncivilized" by the Spanish and they thought it fitting to "civilize" an already peaceful island called "Guanahani" now known as San Salvador, Bahamas. Christopher Columbus and his entourage have been cited in many books as the team who discovered the New World – right. Perhaps it was a "new world" to them because one cannot discover somewhere or something that already exists. The history books whisper the hard truth that this team of conquerors brought smallpox that wiped out an entire people in addition to stealing all manner of treasure belonging to the Lucayans.

Moreover, it was taught in our schools that the West African nations owning large and thriving kingdoms were *"uncivilized."* Human beings – God's people were *"too animal"* to use mere trickery or inflict illness. The English found it more practical to use chains and shackles and ways to ship human as cargo that were fast and cost-effective. Excuse me? Who could be more "uncivilized" than those barbarians of nations who conquered and mistreated the innocent? Surely their stained blood burns corpses and haunts their offspring from their graves!

At the time human life could be sold and justified by those who oppressed. "Supposed Christians" prayed for the safe journey of the slave ships as evil as the conquest of the Arawaks. Why is there never a conversation about that injustice? The alarming question that ties in with divine purpose is if God created us all, how are people who knew nothing about Christianity be thrown into a never-ending lake of fire?

Arawaks who once lived in The Bahamas and Africans who would come to be enslaved throughout the country and the world all connected to what they perceived to be God through forms of spirituality. This connection existed before introduction of "Jesus the Savior." It is said that the Arawaks believed in Zemis, the Creator of a form of spirituality that included worship of nature, ancestors and use of protective magic. The West Africans practiced indigenous spirituality of many varieties, too.

It is important to remember that Christianity was introduced by the conqueror based on the gospel according to Matthew, Mark, Luke and John. A God who resides in eternity who is the Lord of Equality will not have created one people superior to the other.

Who, then, were those unlucky souls worshipping? Satan? It would be outrageous to suggest that they openly accepted Christianity if they knew they would suffer as a result. They had no fighting chance to defeat the forces of trickery, and thus, no choice but to accept Christianity into a trap of unfair fate.

The evil of colonization is the issue. Former Kenyan President Jomo Kenyatta provides a gorgeous example:

" ... When the Missionaries arrived,
The Africans had the land,
And the Missionaries had the Bible,
They taught us how to pray with our eyes closed,
And when we opened them,

> They had the land,
> And we had the Bibles ..."

Being a westerner, Kenyatta's words gripped my belly to the pit. It is the purest form of truth. How does this knowledge tie in with being born with a purpose? This simply reminds me of the conscious lyrics of Ziggy Marley when he appealed in his song "Tomorrow People" that persons who live in the present will not understand fully who they are if they forget their past. This understanding helps me to remember that I am a black descendant of a slave with a history of resilience brought to a country where the Arawaks resided many years later. I am to be all I can be because I am a child of God on my path to fulfill purpose.

A very pure example to share at this juncture is a poem I wrote as a child. Some time ago, I was looking through my closet, and dug up an old English composition book I used in the 7th grade. On a folded leaflet inside the book I found a homework assignment dated Wednesday, September 14th, 1994. It was in my ugly handwriting that I tried my hardest to improve. My teacher awarded my poem with an "A", and it was tacked to the wall among other poems which were also outstanding. A blue star sticker was still in good condition beside my grade. I did the math and it turns out I was eleven. The piece is called, "And Proud of It":

> I am black and proud of it,
> And not for bad reasons;
> I am chubby and proud of it,
> There is warmth for all seasons;

I am a Bahamian and proud of it,
A blessed people;
I am a Mortimer and proud of it,
We praise to the steeple;

I am friendly and proud of it,
No need for strife;
To some this is impossible,
But God is in my life;

A future lawyer and proud of it,
To make the best of my education;
I can't wait to finish college,
For my emancipation;

Not an orphan and proud of it,
I have parents who care;
And a home, to be proud of it,
In a loving atmosphere;

I am loud and proud of it;
Will I ever be calm?
These qualities of mine,
I am proud of them - that's who I am!

The second phrase is made **"on purpose."** There are those of us who want to believe that they were procreated as a consequence of a good night between two consenting parents. Of course that dance contributed, but God brought two people together because He jealously wanted you here. The Most-High loves to be adored. Who wouldn't want to be? You were granted life intentionally because Jehovah desired that we be his prince and princesses to replenish the Earth.

Think of a male who is ready to father his children. I am sure that it can be agreed that a man, when intent on having children, will keep his eyes wide open on the prey until he impregnates the mother to be. There is no difference in the mind of God.

The fact that we can conceive of such a marvelous gift for ourselves with a lover, could you imagine how excited God is when He comes to know what He wants when He creates you? It should be understood that when Jehovah, the King of kings decides to create a thing, it is a perfect thing. Every creation of the universe is distinct and each birth or blossom is deliberate.

Last but not least, we shall analyze the phrase, made **"for that purpose."** Before Yahweh blew life into our nostrils, He ensured that we all possessed gifts and talents.

Without reference to a dictionary, it is presented that there is a compelling difference between a talent and a gift. I believe that a gift is a skill that comes naturally without having to practice it. In other words, a gift is "discovered" not "learned." A talent in contrast is a skill that can be as apparent as a gift, but it is learned. Indeed "practice" makes perfect. A gift is "perfect" and can be modified; but a talent is "perfected" through repetition.

For example, one of my favorite singers from I was a child is Whitney Houston. All humans can sing once they can speak. Words spoken become song through the art of manipulating dust of the air to sound like music to the ears.

So when Whitney sang, the stage understood that she sings, she sang and the lyrics were sung! Period!

That is the difference between talented people who sing by the average ability to maintain harmony and having to learn how to deliver it exceptionally, and the gifted singer who could only deliver it through already-exceptional renditions of choice without apology.

As a former teacher, I have a habit of asking strangers, "What are you good at? What do you believe is your life's purpose"? If reactions could be recorded we would all see possums looking dumbfounded by the shine of a spotlight in their faces and accompanying crickets to signify that they are lost.

It is a very unfortunate thing to live a life without purpose. That is like putting a bouquet of flowers in a vase and forgetting to add water. It is encouraged that we all live a purpose-driven life.

I have come a long way from that Junior High poem, "And Proud of It." Back then, I was a bit short and not so tall, but as I grew, I became wiser, affirming through the, "Mirror on My Wall":

> They may rule the darkness,
> But the Ruler in me,
> Will set them blind,
> By my light, they'll see;
>
> Jail me not in Hades,
> To wallow in my mire,
> Secretly expecting,
> My death by fire;

Angelo D. Mortimer

You can curse my birth,
To be a still-born child,
Binding my steps,
For miles and miles;

But against your wishes,
Like lions after prey,
My indomitable spirit,
Will guide the way;

Just as the stars about the moon,
Alit at nightfall,
My strength is armor,
At war's clarion call;

And like the clouds that drift at daybreak,
Throughout the quieting storm,
My soul regains peace,
When glowing rainbows form;

I am a creation of the universe,
Beyond all seething hate,
The protected of the Almighty,
With a marvelous fate;

Thus my sheer and total gladness,
My enemies so loathe seeing,
Is my crown to be worn,
Such reward decreeing;

To overcome plots of evil,
Standing amidst it all,
Bearing the face of resilience,
Through the mirror on my wall!

The God of Many Faces has gifted us with the power of purpose; may we bask in the authority of that knowledge.

CHAPTER NINETEEN
A Master of Time

"Life is in the moment, and that moment passes by."
– Dr. Desiree Cox, Bahamian Oxford Rhodes Scholar

There comes a point in our lives when, not only do we begin to understand the importance of time, but also value the essence of it. Time lasts forever, and so do our spirits, but we, mere humans, in the flesh, do not. We must die, and so our bodies will fade away. We live in a world that is visible and can be explained to an extent through the sciences. However, there is a world that cannot be seen through the naked eye.

The world we can see is a natural space where all living things known to mankind roam. But there exists a world that is parallel – the supernatural space, where there are beings both beautiful and extremely ugly. That is why some events of life are **"paranormal."** The natural world has exposed wonder in glorious ways and has also revealed the scary. Yet, Earth and all in it cannot withstand the majesty or terror of the spirit world. The heavens are where God and His selected hosts reside, and hell is where evil hosts and other bad spirits exist or are tormented.

I thoroughly enjoyed Biology back in school. A topic I clearly recall is *"Binomial nomenclature"* which tells apart all living things. Quite fascinating is that all creatures are actually named and grouped by two names. For instance, the human being is known under binomial nomenclature as

Homo sapiens which in Latin means, **"wise man."** This wisdom that has evolved over time, in many instances, has become more of a curse than a blessing.

Such wisdom is the cause for many debates because human beings are entitled to opinions and can stand firm on different points of view. There are the many different groupings of people who come together to express their beliefs, which in the name of progress requires that we not lean so much on human intellect, but rather rely on a deeper revelation by "The Higher Source." It is because of mankind and opinions that have led to so many religions as well as their denominations, religious sects and sub-sects.

Mental imprisonment often arises within the boundaries of religion due to the inflexibility to entertain anything other than what is perceived to be correct. It is good to possess conviction, but closed-mindedness should never cause one's affliction to spiritual growth.

For example, with respect to time, it will be agreed that time is a form of measurement invented by mankind – Scientists are still debating the subject. We know that the Creator existed from the past; He is here presently and will exist for evermore. As a Christian, I was taught that the Creation of our universe took seven days. Is this to be taken literally or spiritually? If God is spirit, how is it that we are readily willing to quantify this exact timeline? How do we apply a measurement system of a *"material"* world to understand the timing of an *"immaterial"* God?

On the simple basis that God resides in eternity might merely suggest that God carefully crafted the

Universe as we know it and still is doing so as the world turns. He is God who never changed but is the Creator of Change.

Another idea of Christianity is the notion of the Sabbath. Christians literally struggle with whether Sabbath falls on a Saturday or Sunday. Does it really matter? Man created the schedule – not the Most-High. He is the beginning and the end with no exact beginning or end so why does the Sabbath have to fall on a particular day? The instruction does not even say that there must be six consecutive days before an actual *"day of rest."*

My interpretation leads me to believe that in a 7-day period, we are to choose at least one day to keep it Holy. I should like to think that the more we meditate with God the more intimately we can get to know Him. If we can grasp that idea, the Sabbath can fall on any day within a given week. What is more a *"Sabbath"* for God can be deemed as consistent meditation in His Majesty.

God's omnipotence does not beg for anybody's time. He tends to our needs based on how we appeal for them. It must be understood that Jehovah does not need us, we need Jehovah. Because He lives in eternity He is constantly with us. The question is do we behave in ways that make it clear that we want His attention? Do we behave in ways that are pleasing and encouraging to the Ruler of the Universe?

Even if we attempt to negate that the Most-High is real, we can identify when goodness happens and logic cannot explain how or why. These are God's blessings. Happenings which occur wherein all manner of logic fails to make sense of them suggest that the Creator has intervened through divine intervention. The days of our lives present scenarios which reveal the nature of God's spirit because He operates through us. This magical experience is illuminated in a famous song, "Circle of Life" from the movie and stage play, *Lion King*, which roar that from the moment we are born, there is so much to do in so little time. Yet the cycle of life is a phenomenon that engages us to find our purpose and place in the world through experiences that are not always so clear.

In retrospect, the passage of time has revealed quite a bit to me. I share three short scenarios that prove that God guides, God uses and God grows.

The Lost Key:

This might seem like something small to many, but it meant a lot to me. This experience formed the proof for me that God is always around even when we cannot see Him. Also, it teaches that when time is aligned, "just right", you reap the blessings. On my way out the door from my job one day, I carelessly dropped the key for my work locker. I had no idea that it was even lost until the following day when I arrived to work. Interestingly, I was having a "human to human" talk with Jehovah in my car heading to work. I could remember driving my car in my spirit of always *"minutes to missing a flight."* What comes back to mind are the words of my prayer that day, and what followed, was the priceless peace of God.

I exited my falling-apart Suzuki Liana. I called him Sunburn because he desperately needed a paint job and often coughed and shook on the streets of Freeport. When I walked into work, I began frantically looking through my backpack realizing I could not find my key. At the same time that my face went blank, a coworker, Cherie, walked into the locker room and asked why I looked so "fright-night." I responded that I lost my key and needed to access my locker for some important things. She asked me to describe the key. I did and Cherie confirmed that as she was leaving work, she saw the key on the ground because she nearly stepped on it.

Cherie further explained that she had given the key to the Security Officer on shift. I do not cancel Cherie's act of kindness. The beauty of God is that He showed up to help when I needed Him. It was not a coincidence. What are the chances that at that specific moment, one of many employees showed up to spare me a possibly stressful day? I do not count it as a "lucky" experience when Cherie could have seen me and did not care to ask me why I seemed stressed. When God shows up, it is not luck; it is a blessing!

A Story about Freedom:

Freedom and I had recently become friends, and frankly, I feel like she could be a lifelong friend. She is not the traditional type who sits at my inner table, but I have evolved to see beyond the outer man. Freedom would strike most as someone with whom you do not play around.

In fact, Freedom admitted in confidence that she really is that way primarily from her past. But Freedom, too, admitted that she has changed. Perhaps her desire to be a better person is what attracted me to Freedom. Knowing Freedom has only brought me closer to the reality that God uses us to bring comfort to others even if through random acts of kindness or words of encouragement in passing.

One day we happened to see each other randomly downtown Freeport headed to my favorite pastime, which is to eat lunch on lunch break from work. I was so happy to see Freedom because I had not seen her in a while. Two of her sisters accompanied her and I met them for the first time. One of them bore a strong resemblance to Freedom. I discovered as we talked that Freedom's mother was admitted to hospital. Her progress was not looking so good, but I was led to tell Freedom to remain strong and that God sits on the throne. Although Freedom smiled at my well wishes and words of strength, I sensed that Freedom was deeply saddened by what she was going through. We left.

I saw Freedom another day, but this time she was at work. I did not expect to see her there. When I saw her and asked about her mother, Freedom informed me that she was more stable, but was sent home to recover. She shared some of the symptoms her mother was experiencing and my answer based on what I heard in the spirit was, *"She needs more water"* with specific details.

Freedom responded that the doctors said, *"She is getting too much water."* I did not feel I should interfere with medical diagnosis, but I know God's voice. Weeks later

Freedom saw me and confirmed that what I heard from Spirit relating to being given insufficient water was in fact the issue. She added that there were some events I mentioned which unfolded the exact way they were told.

God brings closure to the advancement of a global people. There is no respect of persons because God provides peace no matter if you are rich or poor. Jehovah never rates us like fellow humans do, but rather evaluates our heart, soul and mind through the passage of time.

A Lesson on Kindness:

My Uncle Etienne, who many affectionately call, "Max" is a genius – no, really! He is my older cousin. It is cultural in The Bahamas to refer to cousins, 40 years of age or more, Auntie or Uncle.

Uncle Max told me of a story when he was sitting at London's Heathrow Airport waiting on a flight to Geneva, Switzerland. He was quite the traveler. What he found pretty disheartening was that a white man that he did not know from a can of paint was pretty much staring at him for no reason. Uncle Max's friends who accompanied him advised that Uncle Max stop staring so intently at the stranger. Of course, Uncle Max thought why not if the gentleman was doing the same thing. What harm, then, was he committing, yes? Eventually, the curious guy would approach Uncle Max and ask, *"How are your mother and father?"*

At this time Uncle Max thought that he was being mistaken. He did not think that someone who lived so far away would know his parents. The times were when people relied on handwritten letters that took forever to receive by post, when meeting an Englishman would be rare and coincidence was perhaps 20% out of a possible 100.

"I visited The Bahamas some time ago and your mother was so hospitable to me. And your father, he is wise beyond measure", the stranger said. It all made sense to Uncle Max now. He humbly updated the stranger on how they were. During their conversation, the stranger was somehow made aware that upon return to England, Uncle Max was in need of a visa to visit a far off place in Asia. The stranger gave Uncle Max his business card, and instructed that he went to a certain company and ask for him upon return from Switzerland. Uncle Max did just that. Visas and accommodation were paid in full for Uncle Max and his friends.

Such random acts of kindness like those of Uncle Max's parents were *"paid forward."* The principle of *"paying it forward"* is that you do kind deeds with no expectation, and they will be returned to you or your offspring in a time of need. At times the blessings come back the exact way that you assisted someone else. The situation replays itself and the recipient is repaid. Other times the blessings come from nowhere. Paying it forward is a way that the Most-High rewards us for good deeds we are encouraged to do in the religious texts.

We live in a time during which the Creator has allowed strange illness to enter the Earth to shift the dynamics of life. The world calls it the "New Normal."

There is nothing new under the sun. Yahweh has always allowed events to capture the attention of mankind.

What we must remember is that we should never forget God, as He deserves our all. He is jealous and deserves to be because we often allow our intelligence that Jehovah has nurtured within to deceive us. How could this be? I conclude with chilling sentiments in the poetry of these rapid times of change. We are, *"The Strange and the Estranged":*

It's in the frustration and confusion,
We've all come to feel,
While our joy and essential peace of mind,
Lady Corona fought to steal;

By the hellish imprisonment,
In our manmade caves,
With unknown cures,
For widening graves!

Such a global quest to survive,
Do stand 6-feet apart,
To survive bio-terrorism,
How did this even start?

This omen lurks like a Dragon,
Spewing the fire of untimely death,
Upon humanity,
As does carbon dioxide,
Remove the air of breath!

Why is this all happening?
Why are we being caged?
Confined to our homes,
With the feeling it's staged?

Is it the awaited Rapture?
The end-time Holy Jail?
I cannot even breathe!
As I long to exhale!

There has been a sounding off,
A King-Kong of a gong,
Presenting "New-Normal" pillars,
Where the unthinkable,
Has been unleashed,
To relive before-seen,
Sci-Fi thrillers;

Aren't we already reenacting the scenes?
Just look at us,
In these flying machines,
Hundreds of souls aboard,
Their engines releasing toxins,
Waging climate storms abroad;

We are glued to screens of technology,
The asthma we feel, we only heal,
By the snatch of smart-phones,
And the outside world,
Of blues and greens,
Are provided by the drones;

Society as we know it,
Morally depreciates,
Because doing what is humane intimidates!

To think that a wretched soul
Is on the verge of dying,
For strangers to take out their cell phones, and zoom!
To snap it! – App it!
Or better, yet, record it!
And share the impending doom;

Winters are standing still in living spaces,
As human faces remain stuck in a hunch-back pose,
Like when the internet freezes,
And in that moment,
A captured scene,
Stays on the screen that froze;

Many humans cannot escape their best life,
From their 'selfies' in a cyber-mirror,
Mere puppets of vanity,
And not until the battery goes dead,
They lift their heads,
As if to yell profanity,

It is like a second coming,
When electricity is no more,
And the emotions of life,
Are displayed like merchandise,
In a local convenient store;

Singer Louis Armstrong
Sang a song,
"What a Wonderful World",
Could we just sing along?

May we be inspired –
By life's simplicity back then,
Back when,
Families and friends were socialized,
To be civilized,
Because life back then,
Was not so commercially computerized,

Now around the globe,
People have become attracted,
To devices at alarmingly high prices,
Why does it have to be this way?
A world addicted to distraction,
Where being antisocial is the order of the day;

Why, then, should the polite soul say, "hi"?
When treated like a ghost,
By those spooked passersby?

Certainly the training of children,
Begins at home,
But living areas are growing silent,
When was the last chit-chat,
Held in your living room?

A beast roars loud and clear,
Fueling coldness in the hearts of the human race,
Creating a modern, anti-society,
In the hell of cyberspace!

Where virtual businesses and classrooms,
Are becoming the standard way,
And human interaction,
Will become distant transactions,
A cold approach to stay!

So the mortality of the human soul,
Will be challenged,
Since making friends,
And staying in touch with the "fam",
Can be accessed and later locked away,
Through the convenience of a hologram;

Welcome to the days of Avatar,
When human existence,
Thrives on reality jumping the moon,
Taking it too far,

Beyond the days of the Smart phone;
Isn't it all strange?
How rapid times have changed?
That this isolation,
Continues to hit every nation,
And life will not make us feel –
Well … so estranged?

CHAPTER TWENTY
The Author and Finisher of our Fate

"To everything there is a season, and a time to every purpose under the heaven: A time to be born, and a time to die; a time to plant, and a time to pluck up that which is planted."
Ecclesiastes 3:1-2

There will be the best of times, as there will be the worst of times, but despite it all, we must die. So while we live, we would want to remember that all we have is our names, and exactly this moment. The very moment you choose to read these words are moments that could have been spent doing something entirely different. But in this moment, your free will allows you to either enjoy or not to enjoy this period of time.

The Almighty Creator is the Author and Finisher of our Fate. Our purpose on Earth is beautiful, and indeed, life is beautiful. But there is nothing more tragic than a life lived not having realized one's purpose. Once I watched an account of a young lady's near death experience on YouTube. Her explanation of what she encountered was profound.

She mentioned that she never did see God but recalled that she arose to exist in a radiance of light. She added that she was advised that she would not be dying, but given a preview of what dying is truly like. Now her version is exactly that, and it is up to us either to approve or disprove the young lady's account of events.

Relevant to the Most-High being an Author and Finisher of our Fate, she described that she observed a gigantic book and the pages in it were turning back and forth very quickly. When she asked what it was, she was told, "The Book of Life." She was further informed that every choice we make determines how our stories are written and rewritten in the said Book. Thus, her claim was that the shuffle of pages is being influenced by every decision made by humanity based on free will.

And so we should be encouraged to seek answers by asking Our Creator to make our life's purpose clearer so that we can always please Him and be rewarded for fulfilling purpose.

Appropriately, when I was a child a sitcom I enjoyed was, "Who's the Boss?" starring Tony Danza. The show's theme song encourages that there are roads to take and those not taken for the decision is ultimately ours to make. So those decisions made take you to the destination to which you arrive whether good or bad.

Times are rapidly changing and progress requires adapting to the discomfort it might bring. There are talks of a "New Normal", but a "New Normal" has remained constant because every moment into the mystery of the future remains new. We cannot foretell the future so would it not be normal to be new? Agreed, inventions have been introduced, and technology has improved, but the thirst to survive has not. All living things merely exist to live and die.

A point I wish to introduce is a lesson I will remember for the rest of my life and the gifts you receive when you are open to others. The details surrounding mommy's invitation to India is not the essential point at this juncture. Her first trip there surprised me a great deal because mommy is a devout Christian. The whole concept of idolatry makes her very uncomfortable so she is opposed to in-depth discussion involving Hinduism, especially images depicting demigods.

However, all the idolatry in the world could not deter mommy from the blessings that would unfold on her visit. She simply understood that, despite her core beliefs, others are entitled to their views so long as she is respected for hers. She had travelled very far for a lesson that changed her life forever.

The distance she travelled! Mommy's flight from Freeport, Bahamas was about thirty-five minutes from the local airport to Ft. Lauderdale, Florida by Bahamasair. She would then catch another flight from Ft. Lauderdale to Dubai, which was an additional fifteen hours. Mommy absolutely fell in love with Emirates that, too, transported her to New Dehli, India.

Yet, the ingredient that made her stay most life-changing and memorable was her choice to live among the locals as opposed to staying at a hotel. Among the locals she unofficially adopted my sisters Nicki and Mina who made an indelible impression on mommy's heart and even mine based upon the wonderful stories I heard. Befriending perfect strangers also shielded her from going blind. Sometimes the people we despise are angels in disguise.

Many of you might not know that India and Pakistan once formed the country Hindustan and was broken apart by religion. The ugly head of religious intolerance rose between followers of Islam and Hinduism causing war and bloodshed. Pakistan remains Muslim and India remains Hindu. It will not be accurate to suggest that people of either religion do not peacefully coexist among each other in either country, but it is a relevant fact in history to consider.

Deeply intriguing to me was mommy's discovery that her passion for God was strengthened in India – a nation under Brahma. Over several trips she became better acquainted with a Pastor who had been delivered from a life of a thunder-rebellion. Apparently back in Nigeria he was a drug lord and womanizer and lived life dangerously. It would be his fate that he would be caught, arrested and imprisoned in Portugal for some nine years as a felon.

After his release he went to India via Pakistan where it could not be believed that he had been so powerfully transformed by friends. Apparently, when he went to India, he sacrificed himself for several months to the wilderness where he is reported to have prayed passionately to develop a unique relationship with the Most-High. When he returned to civilization, he started a small church that became the current ministry mommy grew to love.

On her many visits mommy also observed the racial discrimination and injustices suffered by Nigerians at the hands of all manner of Indian people. Tragically, some of them do not even appreciate themselves either. Darker-skinned Indians are silently scorned by their own people. All races are guilty of this same racism, prejudice and stereotypes that could be alleviated by connecting to Our God of Agape.

In the Land under Brahma, among all its idols, and demigods, there is still God who demands that we love. Perhaps this is the reason why Christian hallelujahs are most felt in churches where churches are outnumbered by temples of Hinduism. When our access to Jehovah is easy, it is easy to take the access for granted. Life goes on – indeed, life must go on since God is a giver of life.

> *"For God so loved the world, that He gave his only begotten Son, that whosoever believed in Him should not perish, but have everlasting life."*
> John 3:16

From a child, I always reasoned that if God and Christ Jesus are one and the same, it does not matter if you are monotheistic (believing only in God or higher being) or polytheistic (believing in God or higher being and possible deities); what matters is that you believe in God or the God of gods – capital "G", as our universal Creator.

Thus, the discussion of death must follow because life will be lived but death is inevitable. There are many thoughts on this issue. God is a giver of life and life everlasting. I do not believe that hell is some endless lake of fire, but is a necessary place we might experience during the spiritual transition of death to the other side.

Remember, the soul of a man is attached to the body and so intellect and all memory of good and evil is attached to it. Our spirit man can be likened to a battle of the spirit, the highest and purest version of self, against soul. The soul, thus, is that part of us which is closest to our carnal nature. The mystery of death can only be revealed at the point of death.

There is the theory of past lives and, thus, the possibility that reincarnation is real. In support of this view is the reference to the words, "everlasting life" as expressed in John 3:16. It can be interpreted as "many lives to come." "Everlasting" suggests forever and not necessarily in torture.

By now you will have learned about my friend Nouria. Being born in the Democratic Republic of Congo (DRC), formerly Zaire, she did mention, as our friendship strengthened, very gripping accounts of spirituality inherited through Zaire-Congolese culture.

Recently during one of our long, healthy and constructive discussions by phone, Nouria shared a particularly enlightening set of events that never left my mind. I asked her if she would mind my sharing the experience that I deem to be a timely contribution. Of course she said no.

Nouria explained that she had a dream and believed God was informing her that she was about to die. Indeed, nobody wants to hear that like, *"pardon me, you said die"*? So she asked that God clarify because she found herself in a type of quarter-life crisis. *She was finna' die, ya'll!* Indeed, Nouria was laughing at this point of her recap.

But seriously, imagine being troubled by that news. As she dreamed, her mind's eye was brought to an album and Nouria could see pictures of herself more recently finding that her death was fast approaching. Her spirit man somehow began to accept that it was her. But what began to baffle Nouria is that her pictures were headed toward the times, decades and eras during which she knew she could not have been born. She awoke …

Unfortunately, Nouria would learn that her grandmother, Rebekah, had died. Well to this point, there is nothing unusual correct? Precisely, but the following is borderline creepy! Nouria's middle name is Rebekah and so leading up to Nouria's grandmother's death, and consequent trip to Kinshasa, DRC, many strange things were taking place déjà vu between Rebekas.

But the event that would stand out was the day her grandmother was buried. According to Nouria, she and family members, as well as family friends, were walking through the cemetery after the funeral. Because Nouria is a short, young woman, she fell behind many others as they walked together. Yet the only person that would guide her was Nouria's grandmother's caretaker who rescued her from feeling hopeless, lost, and neglected. Nouria shared that she would finally arrive at the grave into which she saw her grandmother being lowered. Eventually, the family would again walk, altogether, to the dearly departed's mother's grave where Nouria reports falling and wailing something awful.

Nouria reported she felt like spirits were reuniting. She strongly expressed that until she was able to release bottled emotions at that final grave, she carried a very heavy spiritual burden. As Nouria and I discussed the sequence of events, the caretaker of the deceased seemed to have been so oddly present. It began to invite an air of even creepy. T'was the mutual thought that the caretaker rescued *"two Rebekas"* soul-tied from feeling lost and neglected during life and death.

Could it be that our stories are retold time and time again? Could it be that Nouria's ultimate breakdown was a way for her great-grandmother to transition into another dimension? We know that soul and spirit never die so nothing really changes under the sun. Rather it can be a series of different events over time – same souls, different bodies.

Who is to say many heavens don't actually exist out there? Life is certainly beautiful through the good, the bad and the ugly. Sometimes we must endure the most dreadful experiences during the worst of times, but should always aspire to see the good as there will, too, be the best of times. My poem, *"Reach for Rainbows"*, gives the advice:

> Reach for rainbows after the rain,
> As the moon finally sets;
> To usher in another sunrise,
> The saddened soul forgets;

Angelo D. Mortimer

Flowers are still blooming;
Despite wild weeds,
Set to strangle them — their seeds,
Born of jealousy and evil spirits festering with envy,
Secretly looming;

And with the certainty of tides,
You can gaze to the horizon,
That divides the ocean,
Meant for casting burdens;
From blackening skies,
When heaviness comes again,
To fill your teary eyes;

Every day was not made,
To gain your pot of gold,
But from times of old,
The broken have overcome,
Cultivating the hope,
That we, too, will conquer
Our darkest journeys of fears,
Onward throughout the worst of nightmares!

Endeavor to chase pleasant dreams,
With faith from as small as mustard grains,
Sown into enriching soils of heart,
Removing mountains by faith,
Looking up for a change,
And out yonder will reveal your harvest;

This is the path for which our souls long,
The road to inner peace,

> Even when the Devil,
> Or so he thinks, says, "no";
>
> Might you press with all your might,
> Reaching, in a graceful dance, for rainbows,
> Far away from the depths of sorrows,
> Stepping leaps abound and strides ahead,
> On your quest for fortifying tomorrows.

As the world turns, it is my hope and my blessing that we live in the moment, for all we have is this moment. We inevitably will die tragically, or suddenly, or even smoothly as falling asleep. Yet, in any event, we can die in peace having lived moments before in love.

May we coexist richly in the abundance of life remaining mindful that we are equal – and if we have not yet realized this sacred truth of love and oneness, my passionate prayer is that, as we die daily to this world, we will have learned we are all one people – wondrously created by, **The God of Many Faces** ...

About the Author

Angelo D. Mortimer is a native Poet and rising Author from Freeport, The Bahamas. He received his formal education in Law, but pursued people-oriented fields in Education, Hospitality and Customer Service. Mortimer's most recognized, poetic works include, "Bimini at Ebb Tide", "46 Lit Candles", "Swallow Me" and "We Bury the Dead." The Writer enjoys travel, music, the Performing Arts and tasty food. He says his deepest desire is to greater impact the world through his gifts of motivation and expression. Mortimer is unmarried with no children, but adores his only niece and nephew, Khaleesi and Triston Isaacs, and two godchildren, Eguavoen Igbinobaro and Sariyah Curtis.

Angelo D. Mortimer

Angelo D. Mortimer

www.ingramcontent.com/pod-product-compliance
Lightning Source LLC
Chambersburg PA
CBHW070635160426
43194CB00009B/1474